# Don't Shoot from the Saddle

## Chronicles of a Frontier Surgeon

D. A. Holley

Heritage
House

Holley, D. A. (Donald Alexander), 1924-2000
    Don't shoot from the saddle

    Includes index.
    ISBN 1-894384-08-3

    1. Holley, D. A. (Donald Alexander), 1924-2000 2. Physicians— British
Columbia—Cariboo Region—Biography. 3. Physicians—Yukon Territory—
Biography. 4. Frontier and pioneer life—British Columbia—Cariboo Region.
5. Frontier and pioneer life—Yukon Territory. 6. Cariboo Region (B.C.)—
Biography. 7. Yukon Territory— Biography. I. Title.

FC3845.C3Z49 2000    971.1'7504'092   C00-910933-1
F1089.C 3H64 2000

First edition 2000, reprinted 2001, 2004, 2007

Heritage House acknowledges the financial support for our publishing
program from the Government of Canada through the Book Publishing
Industry Development Program (BPIDP), Canada Council for the Arts, and
the British Columbia Arts Council.

Cover and book design by Emily Jacques
Edited by Emily Jacques

HERITAGE HOUSE PUBLISHING COMPANY LTD.
Unit #108 – 17665 66A Ave., Surrey, BC V3S 2A7

Printed in Canada

The Canada Council | Le Conseil des Arts
for the Arts | du Canada

I dedicate this book to my wife Judith, who was always there when I needed her, and to my kids.

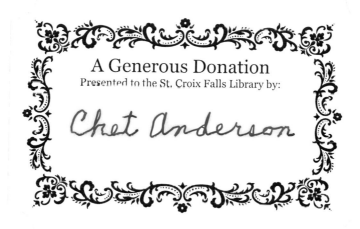

A Generous Donation

Presented to the St. Croix Falls Library by:

*Chet Anderson*

# Acknowledgements

I would like to thank my friend and neighbour Lynn Wiwchar for typing and retyping the manuscript, and seasoned author Dr. Eldon Lee for various little tips on writing and publishing a book. I give posthumous thanks to the late Jerry MacDonald, former editor of the *Cariboo Observer* who gave me help wherever he could. I also thank Chris Thomas and Cam Mowatt for their help when I was never so helpless.

# Contents

# Foreword

Anybody worthwhile will like this book, but it will be particularly welcomed by Al Holley's numerous hunting, fishing, joke-telling, riding and drinking companions. We got worried about him what with so much of his time being taken up with stitching up people in Montreal, New York and Tuktoyaktuk, heading the B.C. Surgical Society, forming an intensive care unit in Quesnel, serving on the hospital board and so forth. Some of us were beginning to wonder if Al would ever do anything with his life.

Well he did. He has written it all down, but unfortunately he was not able to return to the serious matters of hunting, fishing, horse breaking, drinking and so forth.

As for telling stories, he's done it well here. It's a story of high spirits in the low, dark days of the Depression. With an extraordinary gift of recall, he tells of life in the prairie dust bowl where he was born, moving to Cariboo while it was still The Cariboo and the place where he so clearly belonged in the first place, and the struggles to get through medical school without any money. As he tells it, it was all fun. Also, without betraying confidence, he tells of some of his patients who were as freewheeling as he was.

Good for old Al.
I've drunk to his health on roundups,
I've drunk to his health when alone,
I've drunk to his health so damn many times
that I've pretty near ruined my own.

Paul St.Pierre

*On the Holley farm, we mastered the art of breaking horses at an early age. I rode this three-year-old filly when I was eight years old.*

# ONE

# Lucky Lake, Saskatchewan

*Donald Alexander Holley's earliest recollections were filled with dust storms, clouds of grasshoppers, hailstones—and heartbreak when the wheat was all planted and the rains never came, but poverty did. He was born March 18, 1924, in Saskatoon and spent his early childhood on a wheat farm at Lucky Lake, in the heart of the Saskatchewan dry belt. Alex was the youngest of seven children; his parents, Robert and Kate Holley, came out from Ontario like many others to make their fortune from the fields of waving grain.*

*The first few years of life on the prairies, not too long after the buffalo disappeared, were not too bad. There was enough rain to make the grass grow in the coulees for pasture, and although life was tough for the Holleys in this country, there was always feed for their animals, and grain would grow when they broke up the prairie sod and finished the seeding. All farming was done in those days with horses. The Holley farm always had twelve to twenty head of work horses and the neighbours the same.*

Sixty to seventy years later I cannot remember the names of all the neighbours, but I remember the names of all their horses as well as our own. We owned Skip and Tony and Rex and Dan and Dixie and Minnie, and others; one of our neighbours had Barney and Jess and Tony and Daisy; another neighbour owned Ned and Topsy. Some names, like that of a saddle horse, Studebaker, were quite imaginative. We always kept a couple of teams of Standardbred fast-trotting horses.

In the wintertime, when the roads were impassable for motor cars, my brother Art would hitch up a team and drive the doctor and the Mounties on emergency calls far out in the country, sometimes to

*Dad, my brothers and our neighbours take a break to play a favourite horse rancher game—horseshoes (from left to right) Art, Bill, Dad, our schoolteacher Archie, and our neighbour, Harold.*

mysterious destinations away out in the Great Sandhills or the Coteau Hills west and north of Lucky Lake. They would often stay overnight with farm people and come back in the morning. Art told great stories of these adventurous trips.

Horses were always a part of our life. I learned to ride when I was four years old and was driving a six-horse work team in the fields when I was twelve. My dad and all my brothers were good horsemen. Every spring we would have a little rodeo where my brothers and neighbour boys would break three to four work-horse colts to ride. These four-year-old Clyde and Percheron colts could sure buck. My brothers always seemed to think it was good for these big broncs to be broke to ride as well as to drive. At least it was good entertainment. So on a Sunday afternoon a bunch of the neighbourhood would-be cowboys gathered round and saddled up some of these big colts. Since we were grain farmers, not ranchers, we did not have bucking chutes or corrals or a bucking arena on our farm, only the wide-open prairie. They would halter these colts, tie a foot up or ear them down, and get a saddle on. Then somebody would tie a long lariat rope to the halter and put a dally round his saddle horn; the designated bronc buster would climb on; and it would be spur 'em hard and high and let 'er go the way she looks. Our parents or sisters never stuck around for these sometimes hairy performances. They were a little hazardous, but us kids wouldn't miss it for anything.

Over the following weeks my dad and my brothers would break the colts to drive on a wagon with the help of a "Running W" hitch—a harness with hobbles that would trip up the colts if they started to misbehave. A few trips hauling grain to the elevator or dragging a fourteen-foot disc back and forth across a field would settle them down for work. It was always a source of entertainment for us kids when during the course of spring work some outfit had a runaway. They would go across the prairie just a-running and a-kicking and stirring up a cloud of dust that you could see for miles, usually after a line broke on a six- or eight-horse hitch—leaving no way to steer or stop the outfit.

On moonlit mild winter nights we would sometimes rope and ride a few steers and calves just for fun. I will never forget the first Holstein calf I got bucked off—I landed flat on my back and had the wind knocked out of me. I thought I would never get another breath of air into my lungs again. But I did and I have been breathing ever since.

Another great event in the humdrum of a young prairie kid's life was when the herd went through every spring. Some cowboys gathered up all the non-essential horses and all the young stock, both horses and cattle, and drove them out west to land around Kyle and the Matador Ranch—destinations that were mysterious to us kids, as were the cowboy heroes who drove the stock. There were the Jensens. One of the Jensens tied his horse up in our barn and all us young kids had to go and look it over—from a safe distance: the pretty little mare had been said to squeal, scratch, kick, and bite. We took the owner's word for it. All of those guys' horses were pretty good stock horses, and those were darned good cowboys too. They had to cover I-don't-know-how-many square miles of prairie farmland and dig out all the yard-bound young stock from the various farms, force them away from the others, and try to form a cohesive travelling herd. Boy, it took some work and hard riding.

In the fall, after a summer of grazing, the herd came back down the country road, and then the cowboys would cut out the correct animals and return them to the farms they had left the previous spring. The teacher used to let us out of school to watch the herd go by. We had enough brains to not interrupt the cowboys' work. We were usually spellbound. I don't know how the various animals were identified, probably with ear tags; I don't remember any complaints of any stock getting lost.

## Chewing Tobacco

One day when I rode into town for the mail, I was supposed to pick up a plug of chewing tobacco for Dad, who was discing on a half section alongside the road to town. As I was riding toward home and Dad's eight-horse outfit, I began to get interested in that plug of chewing tobacco. When I loosened the tie on the bag that held the mail and the plug of tobacco ("Club" was his favourite brand), the tobacco gave off an enticing aroma. I thought he wouldn't miss just a little, especially if his eyes were plugged with dust from the field, so I nibbled a little off the edges of the plug. It tasted not too bad. I had a pretty large wad of tobacco going and was chewing away like any old farm hand. But I forgot to spit.

When I got about a quarter of a mile from Dad, I started to feel a little unwell. I spit out the wad of tobacco, which by now had started to taste not so good, and I rode on. By the time I got within hailing distance of Dad I was not just a little unwell, I felt bloody awful. Geezus, I felt sick. I didn't throw up, but by the time I got up to him, the field was rotating one way and the eight-horse outfit was going round and round the other way, and I was clutching my saddle horse's mane in a desperate effort to stay on top.

I handed Dad his plug of tobacco and without a word turned my horse around and headed across the prairie for home. Dad didn't say a thing; he didn't need to. I rode to the barn without stopping at the house, let my horse go in the pasture, and lay down on a pile of straw until suppertime. By the time I walked to the house and had a drink of cold water, I felt a little better. Dad never did say a thing to me about my departure from the field, but I imagine he must have smiled to himself. That was the last and only time I chewed tobacco.

## Keeping Warm

When it came to a choice between keeping warm and observing aesthetics, we didn't have much choice when survival was involved. In the fall my dad and my brothers would haul many stoneboat loads of horse manure from the large pile behind the barn and bank it up against the base of the house, all around, to a depth of two to three feet. We left openings for doorways and kept it below the window-line. Later on in the winter the manure began to rot and generated heat so that the floors were warm except at the doorways. During spring thaw the occasional waft of horse manure drifted through the house, but it never seemed to bother anybody. Cow manure or pig shit would never have been tolerated, but horse manure, well, it was just part of the lifestyle of a horse farmer.

We used to burn coal hauled from Estevan or Weyburn or somewhere. Our coal shed was a shanty-roofed lean-to on the south end of the house, which as well as coal storage acted as an outside porch with a storm door to keep the winter wind from blowing against the kitchen door. This lean-to also provided shelter for the dogs and cats. The coal pile seemed to have an irresistible attraction to the cats for their bowel habits. Toward the end of a long winter it was hard to tell whether we were burning mostly coal or cat shit.

*I went to the Lucky Lake School, about a quarter-mile from the farm. These are my classmates during elementary school (I'm on the far right). In Grade 8 I also became the school's janitor.*

Those prairie winters were really cruel. When I was in Grade 8, the last year we were on the prairie, I had the job of doing the janitor work and lighting the fire in the school furnace every morning. I got $1.50 per month. We lived about a quarter of a mile from the school. When there was a bad winter blizzard blowing and you couldn't see 30 feet in the drifting snow, we had to follow the barbwire fence from the schoolyard to our house to keep from losing our way on the bald prairie.

Even though the school was pretty cold when I got there in the morning, I remember how I was always glad to get in out of the bitter wind. Then I had to get a wood fire going first and gradually bank it up with coal. The ink in the inkwells, which we used then, was always frozen, but by the time the teacher and kids got to school it was passably comfortable. The outdoor privies were a long run from the back door of the school, and I tell you, some of those older girls in school could run, especially on a cold day. Some of them would test out Roger Bannister on a short run. Of course they would not do so well on marathon stuff, because there is a limit to how far you can run while holding your urine.

*Uncle George was my introduction to the Cariboo and frontier living. He taught my brothers and me how to hunt and make bannock. This big black bear was killing sheep.*

## Time to Leave the Dust Bowl

The summer of 1937 was pretty awful. There wasn't a drop of rain to be had, and the crops that were seeded in the spring just shrivelled up. The cattle and horses spent their time trying to pick enough green Russian thistle to keep from starving to death.

Brother Bill hitched a freight train back from the winter in B.C. to help with the seeding. He had spent part of the winter working in government relief camps and part of the time staying in the mountains with our Uncle George. George was a bachelor and frontiersman up on Knouff Mountain, where he had a homestead. He grew a good garden, especially potatoes and turnips. Venison was plentiful, and he cut cordwood to sell in Kamloops, 30 miles away. George used to take up a homestead out in the boondocks, clear it by hand, seed it down to timothy hay, and then sell. He would then tackle another piece—a tough way to make a living!

Some of the logs he used when burning out stumps would almost make you cry in this day and age—clear fir 80 and 90 feet high to the first branches and straight as an arrow. He used to tell us of skidding big logs on Vancouver's Granville Street in the 1890s, but there was not much of a market for timber once you got away from the coast.

*Uncle George splits cordwood on his farms. Some of the logs he used to burn would almost make you cry in this day and age.*

My oldest brother, Harvey, made his way up to the Cariboo and was working in 1935 as a hardrock miner in the gold mines at Wells. By the 1930s the placer mining gold rush in Barkerville had pretty well petered out, but the town of Wells, six miles away, enjoyed a boom in hardrock mining. The Cariboo country was one of the few places in B.C., or Canada, where the Depression was not so severe. My oldest sister, Ella, and her husband, Vic Jones, had loaded up their scanty possessions and their kids and moved to Northern Saskatchewan where there was work in logging camps. My next sister, Edith, caught a ride to Trail, B.C., and got a job there. Only my sister Freda, brother Bill, and I were left at home, along with our parents.

My mother had just returned on the train from Saskatoon, where she had her second radical mastectomy for breast cancer. My mother's recovery from cancer—twice—must say something for the good quality of surgery provided by those surgeons in Saskatoon at that time; Dr. Monro and Dr. Alexander, I recall, were two of their names. Her malignant tumours occurred fifteen years apart, but the doctors said the outbreaks were unrelated. My mother lived to age 78 and died of heart disease, not cancer.

But Mother's illness just added to the general depression and unhappiness with our situation at Lucky Lake. We held a family council and the decision was made to move out. Art made a deal for us to move onto an abandoned farm on Knouff Lake, nine miles up the mountain from the CNR siding of Vinsulla on the North Thompson River, and a few miles south of Barriere. The farm used to belong to Art's boss, Fred Casey, who owned Knouff Lake Lodge at the opposite end of Knouff Lake. There was a fairly good house and some usable old farm buildings; a trout creek with good, clear water; a hay field, although the fence needed fixing; and grazing for the cows.

Moving to Knouff Lake meant leaving the farm and selling our horses, which grieved all of us except maybe my sisters. Dad dealt a nice little team of driving horses, along with some cash, to an old Scottish horseman for a pair of four-year-old, unbroken, purebred Clydesdale mares, which we would take with us. We also got a two-year-old Belgian gelding in a trade. Bill, Art, or maybe one of our neighbours reported seeing one of our horses later pulling a delivery wagon in Vancouver. Another Lucky Lake horse was also recognized later in Saskatoon.

A concession that I did not really appreciate enough at the time was the decision to take Goldy, my three-year-old Standardbred saddle horse, which I had already broke. If we could not have taken her I would have accepted it without making a fuss, as we were all doing our bit and that would have been my small sacrifice.

Dad received enough from selling the horses and whatever else he could peddle to make a deal with the CNR. We rented a railway freight car to haul our settlers' effects from Lucky Lake to Vinsulla, which cost about $300, I think, and also included the privilege of sending one man to ride in the car to look after the livestock. That would be my brother Bill.

After it became known that we were pulling up stakes, the neighbours got busy and organized a farewell party. I cringe at the memory of it. The neighbours all turned out, men, women, and children. Friends and acquaintances came from miles around. A local pickup orchestra supplied the music, and everyone danced up a storm until midnight. Then they got our family seated at a table in the middle of the dance floor. They sang "For They are Jolly Good Fellows" and "Auld Lang Syne" and everybody cried and there was no place to hide—Lordy, I would have given something for a crack in the floor big enough to crawl through. Except that he was a Christian Temperance Union man, I bet my dad would have got drunk for a week just to get that tearjerking performance out of his mind. I think that the dogs would have all been howling too if they had been there.

The prairies, with all the adversity of living in those tough times, made good people, and their show of affection was real. By this time in the Depression, what with drought and crop failures, the exodus of farm families was steady and the farewell parties were frequent.

After the party was over it was time to get moving, as there was lots to do. My brother Art quickly finalized the details for our arrival at our new home. Art had a big team of Percherons to haul our farm equipment and furniture nine miles up the mountain to the farm. His boss, Fred Casey, would use his pickup truck to haul stuff, and we would lead the unbroken horses and drive the cattle up the mountain with my saddle horse and one of Art's. So things were ready at that end.

My parents and sister, Freda, were driving out with our neighbour George Hargrave in his big McLaughlin-Buick car. There was room for them in the car, but it would have been crowded with the addition of me, small as I was. So the logical place for me to travel was with Bill in the freight car. That suited me just *great*! Riding in the car sounded like an adventure and was made even better when Bill's buddy, Sid Pinnell, decided to come with us. Our stuff was all loaded late in the afternoon.

The next morning, when the freight train coupled on to us, we were ready to leave our siding and head for Saskatoon. Sid and I were safely hidden up under the horses, where we knew no railroad cop would ever venture. The horses were young but not mean, and it didn't take them and us long to get to know each other. Bill waved good-bye to the assembled well-wishers, and away we chugged down the track on a sunny September day.

## Riding the Rails

We had a set of springs and a mattress slung from the ceiling between the sliding doors and could lie up there and watch the scenery as we rolled along. A pile of straw on the floor provided additional accommodation. It was quite comfy. We had lunch packed for ourselves and the two dogs and two cats. Milking one of the cows into a clean bucket gave us fresh milk for the cats and ourselves.

Macrorie was the first stop, about 20 miles from Lucky Lake. We didn't know what the stop was for, but we knew we were on a siding. Bill, Sid, and I got the idea that it would be nice to have a bag of peanuts to nibble on to make our idyllic voyage even more lovely. So with ten cents in my pocket I jumped over the side of the doorway and headed for a little store just across the tracks. Ten cents bought a good paper bag of peanuts. The merchant was still shovelling peanuts into the bag when I suddenly heard the highball signal, which meant the train was ready to go. I flipped the dime on the counter, grabbed the bag, and was out the door on the run. The train had just started moving and I met Sid halfway to the tracks. He had come to get me when the highball sounded. We both sprinted for the boxcar. I threw in the bag of peanuts and then flipped myself over the half door. Sid was right behind me. We were no sooner in and settled down to serious peanut eating than the train was switched out of the siding and already doing about 20 miles an hour. It would have made an ignominious start if Sid and I had been left behind only 20 miles from home. We did enjoy the peanuts though.

Next stop was at a CNR divisional point, Conquest, I believe. The train stopped there, but we were quite content to stay in the car. Railway bulls (cops) lurked around these stops, so Sid and I lay low, ready to dive under the horses at a second's notice. Bill sat in the doorway and kept us posted. After a pleasant afternoon watching the countryside roll by we pulled into Saskatoon just before dark.

Saskatoon had a busy set of railway yards, with tracks going various directions, row after row, side by side. There were various kinds of trains made up beside us: grain cars, freight cars, cattle cars, coal cars—some empty, some full. Our track was on the extreme left of the main bunch. Bill asked a passing trainman how long we were going to be there. The trainman said we were due out about midnight, and the train crew was stopping to get something to eat at the "beanery" about 200 yards from our track.

The beanery was a cafeteria operated by the railway for the train crews. You could get a hot meal there, cheap and wholesome. Bill was familiar with these from his freight-hopping days. We decided this was for us and we quickly hopped out over the door planks, checked our surroundings, then quickly walked away from our boxcar so that no one could associate us with it. We knew the car by sight, including its number. We also checked our bearings in relation to our train, the location of the locomotive and of the beanery, and the distance from the edge of the tracks. We didn't want to get lost in those railway yards.

Just as we were leaving our Noah's Ark, we saw one of our cats jump down from the car and watched her go under the wheels and head across several sets of tracks. We said, "So long, old cat," and never expected to see her again. We hiked up to the CNR Café (the beanery) and had a feed of sausage and eggs, hash browns, and a cinnamon roll. After a cup of steaming coffee we headed back to the boxcar—still where we left it.

Brother Bill could eat with the train crew and socialize with them on this trip, as for the first time in his career he was travelling legitimately, being in charge of a carload. If there seemed to be anyone watching, Sid and I maintained a discreet distance from Bill, and he maintained the appearance of a cordial disregard for us. I don't know what those train crews thought of a scrawny little kid like me running around the railway yards in the middle of the night. They all probably knew what was going on, but if they didn't care, neither did we.

We got back to the car, climbed in, and settled down. A few minutes before midnight the engineer blew the highball whistle. The train shunted and lurched ahead. At the first shunt a shadow appeared in the doorway—

our wandering cat! She had found her way back across several railway tracks and made a standing jump from the ground to the half door, then curled up in the hay to continue the ride. One of the cows had put her foot through the cat crate and this one cat had escaped, although it was obvious she really wanted to stay with our ark. We slept through the night, and the next day brought us through Edmonton. I was impressed with the rich black soil of the farming country that we passed through, so different from what we left behind. We travelled all day, and except to water the animals there was not much to do, so we curled up and went to sleep.

About 5 a.m., Bill shook me awake and told me to look out the door. There in the distance, in the early morning light, stood the Rocky Mountains: peak after peak, ranged in great rows as far as we could see. There was snow on some of the higher ones. Neither Sid nor I had ever seen the mountains before, and this magnificent sight was almost too much for us to take in at one look. We stayed awake for the rest of the night. We just couldn't comprehend the stupendous sight that lay before us as daylight brought the scene in closer detail all at one time. We must have been between Edson and Hinton, Alberta, when it grew light enough to see this panorama unfolding before us. Little did I realize that the picture we watched was simply the opening page of many more fascinating chapters.

We pulled into Jasper and the three of us hiked up to another beanery for a feed of bacon and eggs with hash browns. After breakfast Bill saw to the animals getting watered, and very shortly we were on our way again. I climbed up on the mattress slung between the doors and looked out at the scenery.

Several miles west of Jasper the CNR branches at Red Pass Junction. One branch splits off to the south down the North Thompson Valley. The other branch keeps on going west past Lake Lucerne and a bunch of other small lakes to follow the Fraser River from its headwaters on past McBride to Prince George and eventually to Prince Rupert on the Pacific. There is really nothing much at Red Pass Junction except the forks of the railway line, but we came around the corner and onto the siding where the train suddenly screeched to a halt.

The wheels had barely stopped turning when a railway cop jumped up in the doorway and said to Bill, "How many are riding in the car?"

Bill said, "Just me. I'm looking after the stock." The cop stood up to get better balance and got a grip on the edge of my mattress to hold on. His fingertips were only about eight inches from where I was lying. I thought he would feel the vibrations from my heart pounding. I lay as quiet as I could, not moving a muscle, wondering if he was going to climb up and look. I knew that Sid would have crawled up with the horses and would be safe. After a few seconds the train shunted and the cop jumped down without further talk.

We proceeded down the tracks, picking up speed. I stayed frozen, motionless for at least five miles down the track before I felt safe to stir enough to look out the doorway. I think one of those episodes was enough for all of us. Afterwards I was sure they would not have kicked a young kid like me off in the middle of the Rocky Mountains at a place like Red Pass. We had no desire to find out, though. We didn't talk much for awhile. I think I may have been too shaky to talk.

The trip down the Thompson River valley was pleasant, with fall colours, nice little ranches snuggled in the valley, and cattle in from summer range feeding in the alfalfa meadows. Occasionally we would see a big buck deer hanging up in a yard, reminding us, especially Brother Bill, that hunting season was open. I think it made Bill itchy-fingered, and he was anxious to get his hands on Uncle George's old 38:55.

# TWO

# Living off the Land

We pulled into Vinsulla with the usual rattle and bang and squeal of brakes. The train crew unhooked us and the train was gone. It was late morning. My brother Art was there with his big team of grey Percherons and a spare saddle horse named Corky. Fred Casey, his boss and the owner of Knouff Lake Lodge, had his pickup truck. Uncle George had ridden down off Knouff Mountain on Punch, his big black mare. He was there to help chase the cows up. Punch was an amazing cow horse, as quick on her feet as a cat in spite of her size—about 1,600 pounds.

Art, Bill, and the rest quickly got the wagon out of the boxcar and assembled so that Art could hitch his grey team to it. The Clyde mares were not yet broken, so they and the Belgian gelding were tied behind the wagon. After unloading, the cows and calves quickly busied themselves getting a bit of grass along the fenceline. Bill, Uncle George, and Sid Pinnell mounted up and started the cattle on the nine-mile climb up the mountain to Knouff Lake. Art and the others got as much stuff out of the boxcar as they could load on the wagon and the pickup. The freight agent locked the rest in the boxcar until morning, and the procession up the mountain began. Fred Casey took me in the pickup truck, and we arrived hours before the wagon and cattle. Fred drove us straight to the Lodge, where Mrs. Casey fed us and put me to bed in an empty cabin. I didn't wake up for supper and slept all night and all the way through to 1 p.m. the next day. I didn't think I was tired.

The trek with the stock up the mountain was pretty long and tiring but went without mishap. Or with only one thing that could maybe be called a mishap: one of our two cats, the male this time, got out of the crate and jumped down off the wagon. We thought we had seen the last of him, but about two weeks later this cat walked nonchalantly into the yard at our new place and made himself at home. Nine miles up a winding mountain road didn't seem to bother him.

We got to our new home in early September and everyone began preparing for winter. There was a plain but fairly new house to live in—it had been the sawmill operator's. We installed our furniture, such as it was—wood-burning cookstove, table and chairs, beds, and whatever few other items we had—and became quite comfortable.

Across the creek, at the foot of a low mountain on the south shore of the lake, were some old farm buildings and a derelict cabin that had belonged to old Dad Roberts, son of the sawmill man. The deserted cabin was pretty messy from pack rats and was not usable. On the door there was this sign, "Don't tuch this dore. Gun set and dinamite." That seemed to be enough to keep people out.

Old Roberts told my brother Art the story of how he and another old-timer, Dad Phillips, were out on the lake in a rowboat fishing and they got into an argument about which way to go. It got pretty hot and heavy until Dad Phillips pulled a six-shooter. As Dad Roberts recounted, "So I pulled mine. The only difference was mine was loaded." I guess they went Roberts' way.

Bill and Art set about breaking the Clyde mares, Belle and Roxy, to drive. They had skidding contracts lined up for both teams once winter came. The young Belgian gelding was only two and too young to break. I helped my dad repair the fence around a twenty-acre hay field, and we threw up a Russell fence, a sort of drift fence, around two sides of the creek and a poplar flat where there was good pasture and willow grouse hunting.

My dad, who was a good carpenter, fixed up the barn and shed when winter feeding started. I never was much good at even rough carpentry, so he didn't bother to get me to help him much on that work. He and I cut up some dry fir for the cookstove to tide us over until snow came. We would buck up the winter's supply with a two-man crosscut saw—no chain saws in those days.

## Not An Ounce Wasted

Bill finally did get hold of George's 38:55 and hunted for the whole settlement. That winter he shot fourteen deer, which were divided between four families with not an ounce being wasted. Bill, Art, and Harvey all hunted, but I think Bill was the best hunter and woodsman of the three, and I tagged along with him day after day up on Knouff Mountain and in other good deer country. He taught me lots. One day on the mountain above Badger Lake we ran into moose tracks, the first we had ever seen. This heralded the first moose that were starting to migrate south into central B.C. in 1937-38.

My mother, in her unassuming way, cooked venison just as if it were prime beef, and it always tasted good. Looking back, it always amazes me how well my parents, raised in Ontario, adapted to the frontier way of life.

Later, Harvey gave me his old long-barrelled Remington Target Master single-shot .22 rifle. Whenever I didn't have other work to do I was up on the fir ridges hunting blue grouse, or else down along the creek hunting the smaller but equally tasty willow grouse. The blues were twice as big as the willows and harder to hunt. They would sometimes take off and fly a quarter of a mile down the mountainside. When they did that, I would take note of the trees they landed in and follow them down. By travelling quietly and carefully I could usually get close enough for a shot when they were perched high in the upper branches of a big fir. Two blue grouse made a meal for three of us. I never did run into any cougar, but with the number of deer around they had to be there.

One time when Harvey was riding on a trail from George's place over the mountain to Louis Creek Valley, his horse started to snort and act uneasy. Harvey looked around to see what was going on. Right ahead of him, stretched out on a big windfall lying above the trail, was a cougar. Harvey dismounted, shot the cougar with one shot, tied the hide behind his saddle, and rode on over to Louis Creek.

Cougars don't take much to kill—you have to hit them in the back of the head where the skull is thin. A lot of cougar hunters just carry a .22 L.R. when they are chasing cougars with dogs.

One dark night that winter a cougar followed Bill and me along the trail all the way from Knouff Lake Lodge to Uncle George's turnoff. He kept 200 to 300 feet above us all along the lakeshore, every once in awhile giving out a bloodcurdling scream. We couldn't see even a shadow of him, but we knew he wasn't far away from us. We didn't have a gun or a light of any kind, but Bill and I each had a hunting knife on our belts. There were two of us, so we weren't too worried. We seldom carried a light in the bush at night, partly because we often didn't have any batteries for the flashlight, and partly because we thought that after our eyes got accustomed, we could see better without a light. Even to this day I seldom carry a light when travelling in the bush at night.

Anyhow, we just kept moving along, getting closer to George's turnoff in the big timber, where a small trail turned off to the right and down to the cabin. We thought this was going to be interesting—the big cat was travelling above us on the right, so when we made a right-hand turn we would meet. Bill and I decided, "What the hell, we'll just let her go the way she looks," and when we came to the turnoff we turned into the big timber and kept walking. I don't know about Bill, but I know I had my knife out of the sheath and a grip on the handle. Nothing happened. I suppose the sudden move toward that old cougar was too much for him to handle and he just took off without another yowl. You wouldn't want to try that move on a grizzly.

The old Remington .22 Harvey gave me sure was accurate, and I didn't waste many shells. I got my first deer with that .22; it was a little spike buck that I got up on the mountain about two miles from home and about a mile up on the mountain above George's cabin. I cut its throat and bled it out, then made a mental note of where I left it and hiked down the mountain to get my saddle horse to pack it home. On my way down I stopped at Uncle George's cabin to tell him of my trophy; he came back up with me to help me dress it and load it on my horse. Old George acted like he was just about as proud of that little buck as I was, in spite of telling me he thought it was a coyote when he saw it lying there on the ground. I was so happy about my prize that I could afford to be magnanimous about such snide remarks.

There is something about getting your first deer or moose or any other big game that is hard to describe. I suppose it must have been like a young Neanderthal man going out and clubbing a dinosaur over the head and dragging it home to feed his family. You get a feeling of exhilaration, superiority, and great satisfaction. Superiority because you went out by yourself and single-handedly felled whatever it was, and the satisfaction of accomplishment because you dressed it out and brought it home for your family to eat (with or without help from your Uncle George).

I have hunted most animals ranging the North American continent including moose, caribou, elk, sheep, goat, deer, timber wolves, cougar, and bear, including a grizzly I nailed between the eyes at 30 paces when he was trying to sneak up on me. I have enjoyed it all and take pride in saying that I never wasted much of anything that was usable. The environmentalists would never understand this. Firstly, most of them are city slickers, at least the most rabid ones are, and secondly, they have never lived a subsistence life where the better you hunt and fish, the better you live. I like to make the distinction between environmentalists and conservationists. I can bet that outdoorsmen like myself have done more conservation work than all environmentalists put together.

## Becoming a Cowboy

I did a little riding for the Wilson Ranch down in Sullavin Valley. Jack Wilson and I were about the same age, and we rounded up cattle on the range and moved them from one area to another where the feed was best. Wilson, Brown, and, I think, Johnson in Sullavin Valley all ranged cattle as far up the mountain as Knouff Lake, some as far up as Upper Knouff and up towards Badger Lake. This was getting into pretty wild country. Jack's

*Jack Wilson (right) and I (left) rode the range on the Wilson ranch in Sullavin Valley.*

and my cowboying took place mostly up towards the north end of the Sullavin Valley. There were a couple more ranches towards the south end of the valley, but they were getting out of our territory.

Jimmie Struthers lived up towards the north end of the valley. I was up there one time when we were baling hay with a stationary baler. I think the family may have had some Native blood in them, not Coast but Cree or maybe Blackfoot. Jim was a tall, well-built man with slightly high cheekbones, dark eyes, and dark complexion. He was a good horseman, and when my family was preparing to make the trek from Knouff Lake to the Cariboo, he shod our team of young mares for us. He was a likeable sort of fellow in his 50s at that time, I think.

Harvey had secured a stump ranch for us at Dragon Lake near Quesnel. At one time we proposed to load the wagon with as much as we could haul (the Clyde mares were broke by then), and Dad would drive the team while I drove the cows behind with my saddle horse. We would go across the Thompson River on the ferry at McLure—that could be interesting. We would then travel up the west side of the river to Little Fort, where we would swing up on Old Trail, originally an Indian trail running up a small creek. We would come out on top of the Bonaparte plateau by Lac des Roches, then Sheridan Lake and across by Lone Butte to join the Cariboo Road (now Highway # 97) at 93 Mile House. We would continue to 100 Mile, then up to 150 Mile, Williams Lake, past McLeese Lake, Soda Creek and eventually to Quesnel and Dragon Lake.

It would take us about two weeks on the trail, camping out on the way. We would take hay and grain for the horses and let the cows graze at night and at noon break. I thought the idea was great and was full of enthusiasm for the trip. It would be just like the cowboys back in Lucky Lake, Saskatchewan.

I don't think my Dad was so enthused. Although he was a good horseman and stockman, he really was not a great camper and outdoorsman. I suspect he wondered how young Alex would make out by himself keeping our little bunch of cows together across 300 miles of unknown country.

The great plan came to naught, however, when a bunch of our stock wintering in Sullavin Valley got into a storage shed that was full of grain. The Belgian colt ate a bellyful of grain, then drank a big drink of water, burst his gut, and died. The two mares both foundered severely (became lame from overeating) and could barely walk. The cattle seemed to have escaped serious harm. Fortunately we had kept my saddle horse, Goldy, at home.

We got the two mares up to the farm and in the barn at Knouff Lake Lodge. There was no veterinarian available, of course, but Dad and Bill and Art worked long and hard on those two horses. They kept hot bran poultices, held in place by gunny sacks, on their whole four feet 24 hours a day. When the mares began to improve a little, Dad and my brothers walked them every day in the cool soft snow as we did not have anti-inflammatories or antihistamines. I don't recall what other measures they employed, but by the end of six weeks the mares were not limping, the swelling had subsided, and there was no sign of the soles dropping away from their feet. The mares seemed to appreciate what was being done for them and became tractable and easy to handle no matter what was being done to them.

When I was about sixteen I was the only one available to shoe them, and they still remembered and held their feet up for me when I was nailing the shoes on. I was still shoeing my own saddle horses until I was over 70.

By early spring they seemed to be recovered. However, it would be pushing our luck to take them out on the 300-mile road trip to the Cariboo, travelling day after day, even if they were shod and their feet looked after carefully. We would need to make other plans. My brothers in Wells made a deal with Him Sing, a Chinese merchant, to rent his big freight truck with a rack on it, and young Tex Enemark agreed to drive it. I was a little disappointed about missing out on the wagon trek, but I think Dad was happy enough. Anyhow, we loaded up our stuff, along with our three remaining horses and the cattle, but this time the two dogs and two cats got to ride in style in Harvey's car.

We left Knouff Lake in good time, arriving in Kamloops in midmorning. We found the brand inspectors' office not far from the stockyards, where we got official clearance to haul the stock through to the Cariboo. I think that we should have had them branded, but since they were our own domestic stock it seemed to be OK. The brand inspector was really taken with my Standardbred mare and tried to deal us out of her, but she was not for sale, period.

Harvey had gone ahead with my mother and sister Freda in the car along with the dogs and cats, all of which were becoming seasoned travellers. Dad, Tex, and I followed with the truck. I still would have preferred a wagon trek, but at least riding in the truck with the livestock was better than travelling in the car with my mother and sister. Tex, who was about eighteen, was already a good driver, and in later years he became well known in the Cariboo and B.C. mining industry.

We made it to Cache Creek, then turned north up the Cariboo Road. Around dusk we stopped at Twilight Lodge on Lac la Hache. I thought that was the most beautiful and peaceful place I had ever seen. Even the name, Twilight Lodge, impressed me. When I drive by more than 60 years later, I still experience a wave of nostalgia when I read the sign and remember my first twilight in the Cariboo country. We pulled off the road and all three of us leaned back and slept for a couple of hours.

We got out and limbered up our legs and then pushed on to Quesnel. We passed the cow town of Williams Lake, then went north past McLeese Lake, the settlements of MacAlister, Marguerite Ferry, Alexandria, Australian Ranch, Kersley, and down the old Red Bluff Hill road into Quesnel.

At the Quesnel River we turned right across Johnston's Flats and up the winding road towards Dragon Lake to a spruce-covered flat and to the stump ranch that was to be our new home. There was a small frame house, woodshed, small fenced yard with a garden patch, and ten acres of stumps. The trees appeared to have been all piled and burned, leaving the stumps sticking up like a giant three-day growth on a man's chin.

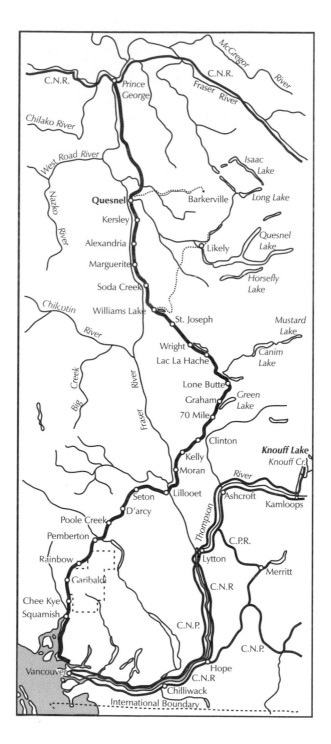

# THREE

# Hunting, Fishing, and Blowing Up Stumps

A haunted house at the top of the hill and a little green cabin were the only signs of neighbours when we unloaded the truck. The abandoned, "haunted" house was at the top of the winding road up Dragon Lake Hill, with a small meadow, which we passed on our way out from Quesnel. The green cabin belonged to George Austin, who had recently been released from Essondale Mental Hospital. I thought, "Great, just great; our very closest neighbours are a recent graduate from a mental hospital and a couple of ghosts. We should be able to have some good parties."

We unloaded quickly, since the poor beasts had been in that truck for 24 hours. We belled the cows and turned them out in the stumps, where there was some grass; the horses we turned into the small fenced yard. We later gave them some grain to help keep them around in case the fence didn't hold. I rode Goldy and led the two Clyde mares, Belle and Roxy, down to the creek for a drink, then chased the cows down for the same, returning them to the stump pasture where we could keep them in sight. We knew that so long as the stock stayed around the area, they would return to the creek for water every day. We got the furniture into the house and some food on hand and settled in. My dad quickly put up a little hen house for our few chickens, and we repaired the pole fence that was around the place so that we could turn the horses out. We turned the cows out on the road allowance, and it was my job to round them up on Goldy every night for milking. We kept them in the stump pasture overnight until after morning milking, then turned them out again.

By following the cows' daily wanderings, I got a good idea of the neighbourhood. Dragon Lake, a half mile away, ran down the hill through a deep creekbed and trickled across Johnston's Flats to the Quesnel

*Don Fullerton and I hunted rabbits around our new hen house on the Quesnel stump ranch.*

River. The creek had a good flow of clear water running in the bottom of the steep, deep bed. At our place the ground on both sides of that creek was thickly timbered. A trail went up past the green cabin into the fir timber. This trail went to the homestead of a wizened-up little Englishman named Bert Tatchell. The narrow dirt road went past our new home to the east side of the lake, where it forked; one branch went up the Quesnel River, the other followed around the east side of the lake where there were some homesteaders living.

There was a good-sized farm at the bottom of the hill, the Carson brothers' place, with large hay fields on the flats where the Quesnel River ran along the east side of the village. There was a place on Johnston's Flats where a Native kid named Eddy Nelson lived later that year. I went to school with him. Alvin Johnson had a farm on the flats where Dragon Creek flowed into the Quesnel River.

I found the trail that went from the top of Dragon Lake Hill, straight down over the creek bank, and along to where the creek came close to the road at the bottom of the hill. From there you could take a shortcut from Eddy Nelson's place across Johnston's Flats to the old Quesnel River Bridge and into town. There was a small auto court, the No-See-um Court, at the end of the bridge. Johnson's Flats were usually good for a couple of grouse when I was hunting. I also discovered a good deer lick part way down the creek bank and stored that away for future reference.

Just along our east fence there was a big ditch, ten feet wide and eight feet deep, which ran from Dragon Creek down to the Quesnel River Canyon about three miles away. Chinese miners dug this ditch to sluice gold-bearing gravel at the lower end of the canyon. One day while prowling around I found that the ditch became a tunnel, about five feet in diameter, at the edge of the riverbank. There were swarms of fleas inside the tunnel, and it was well padded down at the entrance. I guessed some bears denned up there in the winter. I filed that away in my memory too, so that if my mother needed some bear fat for making pies in the fall I could take one of my brothers down there and we could smoke out a bear.

By following the trail a half mile back from our place to where the creek drained out into the lake, I found where the Native people from the Rancherie netted lingcod, which they salted, pickled, and smoked for winter. I discovered I could catch these fish on a fly, spinner, or a berry on a hook. They were pretty bony and did not compare with Knouff Creek rainbows, but were not bad if pickled in vinegar brine in a big crock; it softened the many bones.

I found out that in Dragon Lake there were freshwater lingcod weighing up to nine pounds that could be caught through the ice. Later the next winter I found out from the guys at the Rancherie (like Dominic Charlie) how to catch them too. They caught a bunch of the ever-abundant lingcod for bait, then went out to where there was about twelve feet of water to make their set. They chiselled a twelve- to fourteen-inch hole and scooped out the ice chunks with a dipper. The willows on the lakeshore then provided the makings of a set (as shown on next page).

I used to hike over every day after school to check my sets, which provided me with three or four lingcod each day from freeze-up until the ice went out in the spring. Ling are a mottled dark green and have no scales, so they must be skinned. To skin a ling you first drive a three-inch nail through the top of its head into a log. You then split the skin down each side from gills to tail, then cut the skin around behind the gills; with a big pair of pliers grab the skin behind one side of the gills and pull it right down to the tail. Then do the opposite side. This method will give you two nice fillets. The chickens got the very large livers to supply their vitamins D and A, and the cats got the rest of the trimmings. Freshwater lingcod, sometimes called burbot, have few bones and the meat is white

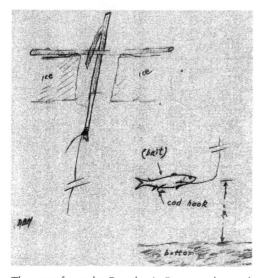

*The guys from the Rancherie Reserve showed me the above method for making lingcod sets.*

and flaky. The fillets can be broiled, or else battered to make delicious fish and chips. We ate lingcod all winter long.

I wandered through little meadow patches scattered through the thick spruce to hunt deer; in the morning and evening one could quietly sneak up on these grassy openings and catch them grazing. I seldom shot does or fawns but waited for a buck. Like Mark Lepetich of Narcosli Creek used to tell me, it didn't seem practical to shoot the brood stock.

There were not infrequently black bears in these meadows, lying on their bellies eating clover. I remember one bear I shot with my brother's 30:06. That bear was about 75 feet from me and I was so jumpy I had to wedge the rifle in a willow fork to keep it from shaking. There were only a few moose around that year. Two seasons later I shot my first moose up on the mountain east of Dragon Lake. Then I spent a day getting him quartered and packed out on a saddle horse. Lordy, that was hard work. I eventually packed the meat part way out to old Bert Tatchell's, who drove in with a team and wagon fairly close to my dad's farm. Then we loaded it up and took it the rest of the way home. I, of course, gave Bert some of the meat for helping me get it home. That was the accepted thing to do.

In these later years I would not shoot a moose that was more than 50 feet from a jeep trail or truck road. Within reach of a front-end loader would be even better. None of this trophy hunting for us guys; rather than being impressed by how wide a bull was between the antlers, I was more interested in its width across the rump. If we shoot it, we eat it.

We quickly settled in to improve the stump ranch. We skidded in building logs and I helped my dad build a good log barn with a hay shed on each end. We tightened up the fences all around and hung gates. Since Dad was an old building contractor in Ontario, everything had to be done right.

We rigged a set of snatch blocks and cables and started to methodically pull out the stumps. The Clyde mares seemed to enjoy this, and although they went through quite a few sets of hames, we gradually got the stumps out and the land ready to break up and seed. The soil was a heavy greyish clay, said to be that colour because of its aluminium content, and was quite fertile. It grew good oats and timothy hay

Some of the bigger stumps—one, two, or three feet thick—got the dynamite treatment. My brothers used to smuggle an odd lunchpail full of dynamite with fuses and caps from the mine. The only trouble with it was the powder they used for hardrock mining was 60 percent Forcite—snappy stuff—while stumping powder was 40 percent and somewhat slower. Ditching powder was only 20 percent and slower still.

*We rigged a set of snatch blocks and cables and started to methodically pull out the stumps.*

*My dad also taught me to plough fields— eventually in a straight line.*

The first big stump that Harvey blew was a big spruce two feet thick. I was out fixing fence about 400 yards away when it blew. I ducked down behind a post and watched this big stump go hurtling up in the air end over end over end—heading straight for the house. I held my breath as I watched it. Over and over it went and finally came down with a thud right on our front doorstep. Two feet further and it would have gone through the front window. Blasting is interesting and fun, but is not for the faint-hearted.

Another unexpected blasting experience occurred one day when we were burning brush in the ditch. We had knocked off the dynamite for awhile until everybody's nerves recovered. The fire was really blazing away when—ker-whomp!—an explosive shower of mud and burning wood flew out of the ditch. We waited until things cooled down before going over to have a look. What we found was a two-by-three-foot pit littered with fragments of volcanic rock, which is porous and looks like hardened black sponge. When this big chunk of porous material got hot enough, the expanded air pockets suddenly exceeded their ability to withstand the pressure and she blew. After that, when we were burning in the big ditch we checked first for volcanic rock. If we could have controlled it better we would have used the stuff to blow stumps.

After a couple of months we had pulled all the remaining stumps and piled them up to burn.

Dad got a good start on breaking up the ground. When he got the horses working well he introduced me to the art of breaking ground with a walking plough. On Ontario farms this was developed to a fine art at ploughing matches, and to see a nice matched team and a good skinner plough a straight furrow was a joy to behold. Through no fault of our horses, some of my furrows were not too straight, though they got better as time went on. Later, when we were breaking up Major Gook's hayfield, which we sharecropped, our outfit even drew praise from the Major himself, who was an old retired army engineer and a B.C. land surveyor. He knew a straight line when he saw one.

Major E.J. Gook was a good neighbour to us, and he and my folks became good friends. He was a tough old British Army officer, and some people thought he was tough to deal with. He was always fair in any dealing we had, and we liked him. Major Gook had stepped on a land mine, I believe, during World War I, and I think he had part of his crotch blown out as he had a most peculiar way of walking. One time he took Mary Ann Donnelly and me on a camping trip up to Beavermouth, and I can tell you he could sure cover the ground. Mary Ann was a schoolmate of mine, a little younger, and quite attractive. It was a very pleasant camp-out.

My mother used to make an occasional pie and other goodies for Major Gook, and I think he found this kindness quite touching. He and his wife were separated, and he did not seem to be close to his family. His wife was rather aristocratic, but nice. I became good friends with the rest of the family and remain so.

Jimmy Donnelly was another colourful citizen who had a place at Dragon Lake with his wife Georgie and daughter Mary Ann. He was the government liquor vendor when we moved to Quesnel, but previously was with the Forest Service and had served in World War I with the rank of

*My brothers Art and Bill worked at the Cariboo Gold Quartz Mine in Wells, overlooking Jack of Clubs Lake (bottom). Harvey worked at Island Mountain across the lake.*

captain. He was a quick-tempered Irishman, an irascible old bugger, but generous, and he appreciated anyone who would do a dollar's worth of work for a dollar's pay. He hired a lot of us high-school boys to work on his place at the lake. Sometimes I drove team and hauled stuff around for him.

Mrs. Donnelly was apparently very well off, having inherited money from her family in the U.S. Jim was very generous (with her money) and that seemed to be fine with her. He also ran a poker club in town, and I believe he took a fair share of cash from various local citizens, especially the Chinese section, which contained many avid gamblers.

I guess he had some pretty hard characters to deal with, too. I recall one day when I stopped in to see him at home when he was ill, and my eyebrows raised when I saw a loaded .38 revolver on his bedside table. I made no comment and neither did he.

Donnellys had a large summer place at Dragon Lake, and during World War II they had several frame cottages constructed on skids, which they gave out free of charge to the young families of service men away at the war. Besides these cottages, he built a big diving raft and various other attractions. For this raft he had a couple of old Swede loggers go up on the side of the mountain and fall some fir logs, 80 to 90 feet long. It was my job to skid them down with our team of horses and drag them into place. He enjoyed seeing our team work so much that he found all sorts of jobs for me to do, like moving these cottages into different locations, the sort of thing you would do with a small cat or skidder if such had been available at that time.

## Bragging Rights

My dad was quite satisfied to hire the team out, but only if he or one of my brothers or I were there to drive them and look after them. One summer I had the team out at Ole Fardal's place (not far past what is now the airport), putting up hay. I cut, raked, and hauled in for that miserable old bastard and did twice as much in a day as either of the two other teams he had hired. Then he tried to gyp me out of my pay. He didn't think I could add. But I could.

Brother Bill worked at the old Tertiary hydraulic mine with the team one season, mostly Fresno scraper work and other heavy hauling. Much of the time they paid Bill to stand around until one of the teams got stuck, and then he would hook on and snap them out. Our team got pretty well known. I often heard Bill speak well of Harold Turton, who was a teamster at the tertiary. I remember Harold for having a snappy little team of drivers and an equally snappy pair of daughters.

Art and Bill were coming home with our team one day when they caught up to Jack Grant with a four-horse hitch on a big load of hay from Nellie Baker's meadow at Dragon Lake. They couldn't make it up a steep pitch onto Hydraulic Road. Jack, who was a good friend of Art and Bill, was going to make a hitch so they could hook in front of his lead team. Art said, "No, unhook the horses to give them a rest." They then hitched our team to the load and snaked it up there in quick time. Art just had to brag a little to Jack about his horses.

One spring day in 1940, A. L. Patchett and one of his men drove into the yard. Patchett was logging birch peeler logs to make veneer for building Mosquito bombers. I guess on that account he thought he was pretty important. He walked up to my dad and said, "I want your horses." To Dad that was like saying, "I'm opening a whorehouse and I want your daughters." Dad very quietly but with great finality said the horses were not for hire. Dad didn't have much in those days to show for a long life of hard work, but he had a reputation for honesty and a fierce pride in the things he had and the things he did. A. L. Patchett was not happy, but he never came back.

## Friends, Neighbours, and Future Patients

Art and Bill came home when they were off work that spring, and during their stay they skidded out a bunch of long fir logs to build a 60' x 40' hen house. They then hauled dry cedar logs from the Quesnel River for Dad to make shakes for the roof. This magnificent edifice held 300 chickens to produce eggs for the Wells market.

My brothers hauled eggs back to Wells when they came down on weekends. Due to the bumps on the road and the speed of their driving, the breakage was sometimes high and scrambled eggs were a frequent menu item at the Holley boys' shack in Wells.

One spring day I came home to find my saddle horse sick. Dad was an experienced horseman but he didn't know what it was. We had no veterinarian available. Next morning when I went out, Goldy was dead. I was devastated. Nothing that bad had ever happened to me. Dad hauled her out with the team and piled a big brush pile over her, which he lighted and burned. When I got home from school there was nothing left of Goldy but a pile of ashes. Neither my mother nor my dad was much for outward show, but I know that they both sympathized with me. I went to school because I had to, but my attention was not focused on my studies for a week or two.

Shortly after this tragic episode in my life I was passing Hill's Meat Market downtown when Lyn Hill called me in. Lyn asked me if I would like a saddle horse, as he had heard I had lost mine. He had a good little mare that he wasn't using much, and I could have her to use. He said he could always get her back if he needed her. I accepted without hesitation and with sincere gratitude.

For the rest of the year I used Mae to ride to school and for chasing cows. She was a nice little brown mare with a white stip in her face and was very well trained and well behaved. I don't know whether he heard that I was a little down in the mouth about my horse dying or whether he just saw the mournful look on my face as I walked by. Anyway, this tough old-timer sure knew how to put a smile back on my face. I rode that little mare a lot over the next year or two and eventually gave her back to Lyn. Some of those tough old cowboys are kind-hearted men.

All of these frontier people became good friends of my folks, and many of them in later years, much later years, became patients of mine when I came back to the Cariboo country to practise.

Many years after that my youngest daughter, Marissa (a.k.a. "Mouse"), aged nine, was without a horse at the Anahim Stampede. We had helped Roy Mulvahill chase a string of bucking horses through the back trails from Chezacut to Anahim, and when we got there we turned the horses out except for the ones Roy needed at the stampede. The other kids all seemed to have horses except Mouse. She was looking pretty forlorn, I guess, when old Dwayne Witte from the Teepee Heart Ranch spotted her and recognized her. He had brought a big black saddle horse with him, which he was breaking and training, between socializing, and he handed the reins to Mouse and said, "Here, Honey, you can use my horse," shortened the stirrups, and gave her a boost up. She was just about as happy as I was when Lyn Hill gave me Mae to use. By the end of the stampede week she had Dwayne's horse neck-reining, doing sliding stops, and pretty well trained for him.

The next couple of years passed by, and I was in my last year of high school. School was not a problem for me, except maybe math, which I had to work at. I brought home a lot of venison, moose, and lingcod during the winter and worked at a few summer jobs, including one as clerk and delivery boy for the Overwaitea store. Bruce Standbridge was the manager.

## Some Call it P.R., Some Call it Smooth Talk

I think I was probably the worst clerk that Overwaitea ever had. I was really still a hillbilly, and my dealings with customers at the store were not too smooth. One day after my response to a woman was somewhat abrupt, the assistant manager, Sid Pigeon, took me aside and gave me a little lecture. He said, "When a customer comes in and asks for a package of mustard or a bottle of vanilla and we are out of it, you don't just say, 'We don't have any.' You say, 'I'm so sorry, Mrs. Smith, we are fresh out, but it should be in by the first of the week, or Wednesday at the latest, and just as soon as it gets here, we will phone and let you know and I'll run it right up to you.'" Sid Pigeon was the master of smooth talk (now called P.R.).

In the '30s and '40s most of the merchants bought gold and took it in place of currency; Overwaitea did this along with the other stores. Only the manager was entrusted with the job of weighing out the gold dust brought in by the prospectors working on the river bars or in some small creek where they found "colours" in the gravel. Old Red Mallin worked a rocker on a bar in the Quesnel River for as long as I can remember. I guess he made wages, but that is about all.

I must have been getting some muscles though, and getting wiry from working at Overwaitea. I used to put 500 pounds of flour on a dolly and wheel it down the street to Cariboo Bakery, where George Allen made the best bread north of Cache Creek.

George did like to take a nip out of the bottle on occasion—any occasion—and he always kept a bottle of rye whisky hidden in a flour barrel. I used to wrap a few loaves of bread for him every time I took a load of flour down. George was a good guy.

## Too Scrawny To Do Much

In my last year at school I had made up my mind that I would like to be either a vet or a medical doctor. I was still too scrawny to make a living working as a logger or a hardrock miner. The options seemed pretty limited.

I had recovered from spinal meningitis, which I had in 1940, the recovery partly by good luck and partly by good nursing care and the medical attention of Dr. John Kovach, who helped Dr. Baker in Quesnel at that time.

In the winter of 1942 I had to get a bunch of teeth fixed. At this point I was so broke that I couldn't afford to pee up against a high board fence at a cent and a half a yard. I had no immediate prospects of seeing any money. My brother Art told me to go and get my teeth looked after and he would pay for it. Thirteen fillings later, all done without freezing, I no longer had a single aching or rotten tooth. And I had become a friend of Doc Sumner, a graduate of North Pacific College of Dentistry in Portland, Oregon.

I had no rich friends or relatives, and if there were anything like scholarships available, I did not know about them. To get your M.D. degree took two or three years of pre-med arts and sciences, followed by four years in medicine, plus a year of internship in a hospital. Dentistry took one year pre-dent, then four years of dentistry and you were ready to go out and make money. That sounded a bit better to me. A little far distant perhaps, but possible. Doc Sumner loaned me his operative dentistry books to look at, and the dental surgery instruments intrigued me. He gave me encouragement but did not have any magic sources to suggest for financing. My grades in high school, except for math, were all good, so I did not worry about making it through university. It was something to think about.

About twenty years later, while working at Bellevue Hospital Medical Centre in New York City, I had to have a tooth looked at and went in to the hospital dental centre. The dentist asked me where I had got my dental work done. I told him Quesnel, B.C., out on the frontier in Western Canada. He was so impressed that he called the professor and chief of Dental Services over, and that whole dental class had to come and look at what a good job Doc Sumner had done on my teeth. Dr. Sumner died without my ever telling him about the attention he got.

# FOUR

# March 21, 1943

That was the way things were going along until March 21, 1943: the day I found my dad lying in the snow at the woodlot. I was walking home from school and took a little detour to see how the woodcutting was going. Dad was lying in the snow, unconscious, with no sign of a tree falling on him or any other injury. I didn't know much about those sorts of things, but I guessed right away that he had had a stroke. We were about three-eighths of a mile from the house, and Dad was six feet tall and weighed 190 pounds. I didn't know how I could get him home.

I got hold of him by the shoulder and dragged him out of the cold snow and onto a pile of brush, then set off at a trot for the house. I knew Mother was home, but she had cardiac problems herself—even both of us together would be unable to lift him. As I was trotting I was thinking that perhaps I could harness one of the horses and hitch it to the stoneboat, drag him onto that, and get him to the house until we decided what to do.

Just as I was nearing our gate, Bill Irwin, a neighbour, caught up to me with his car. I hailed him and quickly told him what happened. He turned the car around and we drove back to the woodlot. Bill was a big hefty logger who worked for Forestry, and we lifted Dad up and into the back seat. After a brief stop at the house to pick up Mother, Bill took them directly to the hospital. I stayed to feed the animals and tend the fires in the house.

Dad lived for a week but never regained consciousness; it gave all the family a chance to get there.

Dad was not demonstrative in his affection, but at home when we were working together he always gave me the feeling that he was there when I needed him and displayed great patience when he was showing me how to do things. In a quiet way we had a great affection for each other, and I had the greatest admiration and respect for my dad. He was buried in the old cemetery above LeBourdais Park, with the other half of a double plot saved for my mother. Things were going to be different, certainly not easier, I knew.

My mother and I kept things going on the stump ranch. My sister Freda came out on her days off from her cooking job at the hospital, and my brothers all stopped in when they could get down from Wells.

People were kind to us, although we were doing pretty well on our own. My social studies teacher, Mr. Murray, walked out from town one weekend to help me when I was seeding. The mares had colts, with no great problems, but during final exams one of the colts was sick. One morning I was tending this sick colt until I was just about late for the government exams at school. I finally grabbed my coat and lunch and lit out the door on a dead run. When I got part way across Johnston's Flats I met the town taxi coming out to meet me. Pat Gwyer, the principal, had dispatched it to get me when she feared I was not going to make it to school for the exam. My mother and I both thought that was very kind and considerate of Miss Gwyer, and it was that sort of kindness that made me return to the Cariboo to work and help the people up there.

I passed all my Grade 12 exams, which gave me my junior matriculation and B.C. university entrance. At that time, in order to gain entrance to the prairie universities as well as most others back east, you had to have your senior matriculation (Grade 13), which you obtained in one of the larger B.C. high schools or in first-year university within B.C.

My mother and I decided we would move to Trail, B.C., where she could stay with one of my sisters and help look after the house, and I would stay with my other sister and do my senior matriculation.

Harvey made a deal to sell the Dragon Lake ranch to Harry and Rosie Gassoff from Saskatchewan for a little bit more than he paid for it. So the stump clearing and building that Dad and I did was worth *something*, I guess. We remained good friends with the Gassoffs, and over time I became one of their extended family—the only Irishman-United Empire Loyalist in a large family of Ukrainians. Nobody enjoys a feed of cabbage rolls and perogies more than I do.

## FIVE

# On The Road

Since it was wartime and they were short of labour at the Cominco smelter, most of us high-school students put in two shifts every weekend. We made a few bucks helping the war effort. I finished senior matric in Trail, and when school was out I hitchhiked back to Quesnel.

Brother Bill had started a dairy farm up there by then, and Freda had married Jimmie Bourne, a construction engineer who was in charge of building the Quesnel airport. Jimmie got me a job calculating yardages for the grading contract until I signed on for the summer with the survey outfit that was staking out the route for the Hart Highway from Summit Lake, along the Crooked River to McLeod Lake, across the Parsnip River, and over the Pine Pass to the Peace River country.

There were quite a bunch of us from Quesnel on the crew, including one of my old friends Jed Campbell: it was like a summer picnic for us two. Dick Corless had riverboats that ran from Summit Lake to the Parsnip and on up the Finlay River to Fort Ware. He hauled some stuff for us. We had a riverboat owned by Andrew Prince of Fort St. James.

I was axeman, chainman, and later rodman on the crew, and sometimes river boatman with Jed Campbell and others, running the Crooked River with our camp outfit. Working with the guys was way better than trying to be polite to Overwaitea's customers. We moved camp every ten miles along the river. We would hike five miles back to where we left off, then would work on past our camp, cutting line for five miles ahead before moving camp, another ten miles. Sleeping in tents and working in the fresh air all day—a great summer.

*Surveying Pine Pass highway with Chas. Edkins (top). River-boating on the Crooked River with Jim Fox , Andrew Prince, Bob Thomson (bottom right). "Hardrock" Holley (me) and George Bogue hard at work in Greenwood (bottom left).*

## Saturday Night Menagerie

I had to quit a little early to get over to Edmonton for the start of university, so I went back up to Summit Lake in a riverboat and hitched a ride to Prince George on a truck. At the first restaurant I entered, this old waitress put her elbows on the counter in front of me and inquired, "Been in the bush long?" She could see damned well I had been in the bush long, and I didn't like the leer on her face either.

After finishing my meal my next stop was a barbershop. I got a haircut and had my lush golden-red beard shaved off. I cashed one of my accumulated summer paycheques and bought a CNR railway ticket to Edmonton. I also exchanged my bush clothes for some clean town clothes. The train left at 7 p.m. At the appointed time I dragged my old suitcase with me and climbed on board.

That was quite a voyage! Prince George and points along the east Fraser were *not* very civilized in 1944, especially on Saturday nights. All the local passengers from Purden Lake to Slim Creek, Dome Creek, and McBride had been to Prince George shopping, drinking in the bars, and whatever. There were loggers and trappers with booze on their breaths; Native families with kids who had peed their pants; malamute dogs—this train carried quite a menagerie. I thought, "Boy, I would like to throw a stray tomcat into the coach with all those sled dogs. Just what we need to liven things up!"

By the time we got a half-hour out of the station, an active poker game was going on, jugs of rye were uncorked, and empty beer bottles were rolling up and down the aisle. Even the conductor had a pretty good glow on and was acting quite jolly.

About midnight I heard a woman ask the conductor to let her know when we were close to Snowshoe, as that was where she was supposed to get off. The conductor said, "Snowshoe! We passed there a half-hour ago. But don't worry, lady, we will wake the man up at the next stop and he will take you back on a handcar." The woman looked like she didn't know whether to cry or hit him with her handbag.

During that trip I made the acquaintance of Goat River Slim. This rather nonchalant-looking fellow sat down on a seat with me, and after we had chatted for awhile he pulled out a twenty-sixer of rye and asked me if I would like a drink.

I said, "Sure, I'll have a snort." So I knocked back a pretty good one straight from the bottle. Slim looked on approvingly.

He had a pull on the bottle and said, "Have another one."

"Thanks. I don't mind if I do," I said.

And with that for openers he began to tell me all about the Goat River country and his experiences living there. He was a trapper and big-game guide, and I guessed he didn't spend much time in town.

Several years later when I spent some time with Frank and Tim Cushman, who guided into the Goat River from the Bowron Lake side, I would have been glad to know more about that rugged, mountainous piece of ground. Tim went through once or twice with horses, and he and his son Brady hiked through in the summer of '98. He told me it was one of the roughest pieces of ground he had ever gone over.

I know an outfit from the Okanagan started through there the same year that Tim rode it, but they only got part way before they turned back because it was too tough. The fact that Tim got all the way through is not surprising. You have to have travelled with Tim to know why. The Goat River is a narrow, rocky, fast-flowing stream that tumbles down out of the Cariboo Mountains, crosses Highway 16, and empties into the east Fraser a few miles west of McBride.

Goat River Slim's stories were most interesting and helped to pass the time. The train pulled into McBride in the early morning hours, and a bunch of passengers got out. The loggers were pretty soused by this time, and there was some pushing as they staggered towards the passenger car doors. One big logger told another one, "Quit your pushing," and gave him a cuff on the jaw. At that point both men were carried on a wave of people out the door. When I looked out the car window I could see a ring of loggers forming under a streetlight and these two big guys were squaring off in the middle of the circle. I would have liked to watch the fight, but the train gave a couple of toots and pulled out—so much for Saturday night entertainment in McBride.

## Adversity Number One and One and One . . .

Late the next day, I carried my old suitcase up to 101 Street in Edmonton and soon came to an old flophouse that didn't look fancy but suited my pocket book. I rented a room for a couple of dollars. It looked clean enough and the bed was made. However, I noticed that you had to go through my room to get to the next room. I was tired and went to bed.

Later during the night, this fellow and a woman, a hooker I think, passed through my room to theirs. They were friendly enough, and so was I. When you are in a frontier town and not too flush, you can't afford to be snooty. They didn't keep me awake; I slept well until morning. I was dressed and ready to go out for breakfast when they went out. Before they left, the man poured me a good drink of whisky in a glass and said, "Here's a drink for you, kid," and he left it on my dresser. I figured I'd need it that day, so I downed it and went for breakfast.

One of the airport construction workers I worked with at Quesnel had told me, "Just look us up when you get to Edmonton. My wife is there and you can stay with us, kid." In my naive way I took him seriously, but when I phoned Jim Fanning's number I was told it was no longer in service, and when I saw that his listed address was away out in West Edmonton, I knew that it was too far from the university for me anyway. So chalk up adversity number one.

I was in a strange city where I did not know a soul, but I was not going to let that deter me. I gave the man at the flophouse a dollar to look after my suitcase and hoped that it would still be there when I got back. After checking a street map I set out walking, up Jasper Avenue to 109 Street and over the High Level Bridge to the university. Pre-dentistry classes did not commence until the next week. I went to the university main office where there was a student-housing bureau. The secretary told me that the dorms, Athabaska Hall and Assiniboia Hall, were full, but she gave me a list of people in the university area who would take student boarders. After getting some information brochures I took the list of boarding houses and set out to find me a place. The first rental was at 111 Street and 82 Avenue, not too far to walk to the U. Just as I knocked on the back door, the landlady was letting in another student by the front door.

She looked us both over and said, "I only have one room and I want $18 a month for it but if you want to share, it will be $9 each." The other guy was George Mathers, an engineering student from Saskatchewan.

He looked at me and I looked at him and we both said, "Suits me." Mrs. Putnam told us that she did not supply meals, but there was a place across the street where meals could be had, and another place three houses down, at the Reverend Finlay's. We tried the place across the street first, where twelve to fifteen students ate. The meals were pretty bad and we noticed that each table went through one large bottle of ketchup per meal in order to make the food edible. We agreed that was not a good sign.

Rev. Finlay's boarding house had both room and board and also catered to just boarders. The Reverend's daughter was separated or divorced, which they never discussed, but she was clean and nice and looked like a good cook. Since she was a very nice person, all of us guys tried to be good to her. We ate there all year. Reverend Finlay was an old die-hard Presbyterian and preceded each meal with a lengthy blessing, more like a funeral service than grace. Each Sunday he took the service at Rabbit Hill Presbyterian Church just south of the city.

In the Reverend's absence, we students all had to take turns asking the blessing. When he was there to give the service he used to put great emphasis on the grand finale, "For Christ's sake, Amen." When we were taking our turn in his absence we used to try and outdo each other in our eloquence, and in a great thunderous voice used to end the prayer with, "For Keeryste sake, Amen!" and in the next breath, "Please pass the potatoes." Needless to say there were no theology students in our group.

# Highway Surveys

The year went well. One of the guys two years ahead of me became professor of surgery at McGill University. I didn't get home for Christmas but got a job with the CPR unloading express cars over the holiday: not a bad job, with good money.

I started looking for summer jobs. There was not much available for untrained university students, but I was lucky. Jimmie Bourne was construction engineer on a Highways project building the Ashcroft cutoff from Cache Creek to Spences Bridge, and he had a job for me.

One of the guys I got to know from Vancouver put me onto a deal for getting back to B.C. It seems that according to the Railway Act, cattlemen from the prairies shipping to the stockyards in Vancouver were allowed a man to travel in the caboose, one for every carload.

Some university student had a friend working for the livestock brokers Weiler and Williams in Edmonton, and those brokers must have been sympathetic to poor students too, as they exercised their right under the Railway Act to send a man with each carload. That is where I fit in. Being a naive farm boy, I fully expected that I would have to feed and water my charges when we stopped along the way. Instead I found that they wanted these butcher cattle to be empty when they got to their destination so that they would be ready for the slaughterhouse. I was really just conveying a carload of T-bone steak on the hoof to Vancouver and never even saw the cattle on the way.

On the afternoon of departure I went out to Weiler and Williams' office at the stockyards and picked up a copy of the shipping bill for my carload. That bill was my first-class ticket in the caboose from Edmonton to the Port Mann freight yards across the river from New Westminster. The freight was due out at midnight, so I had to be there a little early to find the train and get settled in the caboose. One of my more affluent classmates who had a car drove me out to the yards. I found a trainman and showed him my waybill, on the strength of which he led me through the dark to my train. I packed a lunch and a warm jacket. The train crew had a coffee pot that they heated on a small coalstove in the caboose. The caboose had two or three seats that were long enough to stretch out on—they looked pretty comfy to me. I was the only courtesy passenger.

At midnight, right on time, the engineer blew the highball whistle, and after a couple of shunts we headed out.

That was one of the best trips I ever had. The spring weather was balmy, and as we went through the Rockies the train crew and I sat out on the back of the caboose and watched the scenery. There were mountain goats and sheep lying in the sun on the outcroppings, elk on the open sidehills, and moose on the edge of lakes. The trainmen and I chit-chatted: they told me about railroading and I regaled them with stories of ranching and cowboy life in the Great Sandhills of Saskatchewan and the Cariboo country of B.C. We rattled along down the North Thompson, through North Kamloops, and along Kamloops Lake.

I told them I would like to get off close to Cache Creek, as that was where my job was. The brakeman told me that the train slowed down when it climbed up on the flats past the end of Kamloops Lake, and it would be a good place to jump off. When we were just about to the top of the grade, and the engine was puffing pretty hard to make it, he said, "Now." I threw the suitcase out and jumped. The suitcase bounced down the grade and I rolled after it. I got to my feet, picked up my suitcase, and waved goodbye as the caboose rounded the next corner.

I made my way through the sagebrush. The highway was up there somewhere, and I hoped that the rattlesnakes were not too thick on the way. I later found out that there was no shortage of them around Ashcroft. On the highway I thumbed a ride with a rancher in an old Model A Ford pickup. I threw my suitcase in the back and climbed in the front. He said he knew where the road was being worked on, between Cache Creek and Ashcroft Manor, and would let me out there so I could get to work. He found it amusing that I had ridden a freight train all the way from Edmonton to get a job out here. He chatted away and he was further amused when he found that I planned to be a doctor, specifically a surgeon.

He let me off at the work site. I threw my suitcase in Jimmie Bourne's Highways truck, put on my heavy work boots, and got an hour's work in before lunchtime. I even had half a sandwich with me for lunch. We worked all summer and had the project just about finished by fall.

## Picking Locks with an Axe

I think that by the end of summer both our survey crew and the construction crew must have had enough Vitamin C in our systems to last us for a year. There was a great crop of tomatoes growing all around the area, and when the loaded trucks stopped for the construction on their way to the cannery, we each grabbed a couple of tomatoes. Everybody carried a salt shaker in their truck, and we really pigged out on those Ashcroft tomatoes. They are the best, and when the cannery was running, Ashcroft brand canned tomatoes and Ashcroft Catsup were known all over the country. Later General Foods Co. of Toronto bought the cannery and closed it down: that was their way to deal with competition.

We spent the summer on the highway job with no major disasters occurring. We killed a few rattlesnakes on the job, enjoyed watching fights

*Parky Parkinson (centre) and I (left) spent our days off from roadwork riding in the mountains—and lakes. It was a good way to meet girls like Margo Parker (right).*

among the construction workers—truck drivers, cat operators, and the like. Those guys were a pretty hard lot.

I stayed in the bunkhouse supplied by the contractor for workers. Three of us younger fellows knocked around together. Sometimes on Sundays we joined the two Parker girls from Ashcroft Manor for rides up into the mountains. Once you climbed up out of the hot dry sagebrush of the Thompson River valley, the top was cool and green, with little lakes where we took our horses swimming.

One Saturday night Rick, Parky, and I had a few beers in town and were a little noisy when we got home. The bull cook locked the bunkhouse door on us. We really weren't *that* noisy, and we wanted to go to bed. When I saw the door locked I just picked up an axe and chopped the lock off the door. Next morning I thought there might be hell to pay, but when the bull cook went mouthing off to Jimmie Bourne about it and got a little obnoxious, Jimmie clocked him one on the jaw and knocked him on his ass—that seemed to end any further discussions.

## Second-Lowest Form of Life on Campus

Fall came and I went back to Edmonton to start second year. Before I left at the end of first year I saw the Dean of Arts and Sciences and asked if I could switch from pre-dentistry to second-year pre-med. He conferred with his committee and they said I could do it, but during the summer I would have to take, on my own, a course in integral and differential calculus, a university math course that was required to get into medicine but not dentistry. Don't ask me why. Math was my worst subject, but I gulped and said I would work on it all summer and write the exams. How I ever got into second-year pre-med I'll never know, because I loused up that math something awful. I guess the admissions committee thought that if I wanted to get into medicine that damn bad, my motivation must have been good.

At the end of second-year pre-med they culled 50 candidates from the 200 or so applicants, and these 50 got into medicine. I was lucky and very thankful to be among the 50.

In second year things seemed to be picking up: we were now only the second-lowest forms of life on campus. We had begun to find our way around and even got asked out to Nursing School parties by student nurses (mostly first-year nurses). The Putnams moved to a new house down on University Avenue, and since they had extra room in the new place, George and I moved with them. We were by now part of the family. Bob Putnam was deputy minister of Agriculture; his wife, Jean, was a very nice and down-to-earth person; and they had two kids, whom I babysat. (George was in his last year and was too busy for that.)

I soon found my way out to the University Farm, on the outskirts of the campus and spent many Sundays there. Seeing some horses and cows made me feel less homesick.

We were kept busy in classes, and one of the useful things we learned to do in organic chemistry was set up distilling equipment for making ethyl alcohol. We learned the characteristic odour of $H_2S$ (hydrogen sulfide), or rotten egg gas as it was called in the lab. We also learned that in very high concentration you could not always smell it, and in such a situation, if you didn't get out in the fresh air, it could be fatal. In later years we smelled that stuff frequently around pulp mills in B.C. and gas-scrubbing plants in Alberta.

During Christmas exams that year the guys in Athabasca Hall men's residence got shook up some. At a Saturday noon lunch they noticed that there was one empty chair. They wondered who was missing and why he wasn't at lunch. A short time later a couple of RCMP officers showed up to see if there was anyone in residence with a name that corresponded to the ID they had found on the body of a young man discovered on the rocks under the High Level Bridge. A quick check

*The Kettle Valley Engineers pose at Midway, B.C. in 1947: (left to right) Gordon, Freda, Jimmie Bourne, Jo-Anne, Al, Ron Roylance and Carl.*

showed that it was the missing student, who had evidently jumped 137 feet from the bridge and was killed on the rocks below. Most of us didn't take our exams quite that seriously.

A nice young lady from quite a religious family invited me out for Christmas dinner that year. Her brother, Jack, had recently graduated in theology and had just been ordained as an Anglican minister. We all had to take communion, even me. I guess Jack needed the practice in giving the right communion speech. I felt somewhat like the Native people up north at Aklavik, who went to whichever church gave them the best handouts.

After dinner, Jean and I went to a little Christmas party with some med student friends. That was the first time I ever started the night drinking communion wine and ended up on moonshine from the lab. It was "Ho, Ho, Ho and Merry Christmas," and a good time was had by all.

## Pranks on the High Road

The year went by quickly and soon it was summer-job time. I had a job lined up with Jimmie Bourne and the Highways department again. This time it was redoing a section of the trans-provincial highway from Rock Creek to Grand Forks, in the Doukhobour country. We set up camp on the south side of the Kettle River at Midway, close to the U.S. border. We had a couple of crew members that came over from the Ashcroft job and a couple of local boys from Greenwood. Besides Doukhobours, there were some real hillbillies in that Rock Creek-Greenwood area.

About the second night we were in camp, this old Model A pickup truck came rumbling across the bridge. The Bolts boys had come to look

*An opportunity too good to miss—Margo Parker (l), Vashety (c), and friend (r) became close friends with Ron, Parky and I.*

at our camp set-up and to warn us young fellows not to be messing around with their girlfriends. Of course that was a challenge too good to miss.

An American cowboy from across the line used to ride up to Midway to see his girlfriend. When he crossed at the Canadian customs house he had to unload his six-gun and leave it at the border until he went back. He rode with an empty holster in Canada, while the local cowboys, like the Bolts brothers, carried six-guns when they were riding on the range.

I was working as instrument man on the survey crew, and the other boys were chainmen, rodmen, and general utility men. One of these guys was a terrible snorer, especially if he had a bellyful of beer. There were six of us sleeping in a tent. One night he came in drunk and was snoring so loud that none of us could sleep. We tossed boots at him and other things we could throw, but that did not quiet him a bit. Finally Ron Roylance and I got up and put our boots on and opened the tent flap. We took him by the head and the feet and carried him over to an old railroad grade and stretched him out with a rock for a pillow. Afterwards we worried a bit because there were lots of snakes on that flat; however, we decided that no rattlers would go near him as he sounded like a power saw.

General Contracting out of Vancouver did the roadwork, and they were not too efficient. The superintendent accused us of not giving them accurate figures on the yardages moved. The chief location engineer came up. Jimmie had him run the levels on a one-mile strip of grade and then had my rodman and me run levels over the same strip. At the end of a mile we were one inch out from the measurements given by the chief engineer from Victoria. That shut up the whining construction man and gave our crew a good boost. Jimmie got a raise for our survey crew.

We had a tough old-timer on the construction crew. Vic Barrett was his name. He had a cabin on Boundary Creek, close to Greenwood,

*Cliff Kohn, on the "Screaming Six," grades the trans-provincial highway in the Kettle Valley.*

with a buck deer's scrotal sac (testicle bag) nailed on the wall for a toothbrush holder. Someone commented one day about the chain-link mesh he had on the windows. "That's pretty skookum mosquito netting you have there, Vic."

Without a trace of a smile Vic replied, "Well it keeps out the big ones, and the little ones don't bodder me."

Ron Roylance told us of a fight that started in the old hotel at Greenwood. Some punk took a swing at Vic, who reached down, stuffed his fist in a brass spittoon that was sitting on the floor, and drove the punk on the jaw. The guy hit the floor like he had been hit by a pile driver. He didn't even move. Vic thought he had killed him, so he got his things together and never stopped until he got to his trapline cabin fifteen miles up the West Fork. One of his friends went up there looking for him and told him it was safe to come down, as the guy he hit eventually came to.

Snuffy Smith was a kid who had come with his parents from Barkerville and who went to school in Greenwood. He was a wild little bugger. He got hold of a can of Vic's mink-trapping bait one day and smeared it on top of the furnace in the school basement. Vic kept his trapping bait in a jam can. It was made with a couple of dead squirrels, a robin or two, and two or three fish. He then hammered the lid on tight and set it at his backdoor for a few weeks to age. To make a mink or a martin set he would simply break off a stick, poke it into the mixture, and then stick the other end into the snow over his trap. I guess this was pretty potent in the warm weather. A mink could smell it for five miles. After the furnace heated up with this stuff on the top I guess the stench produced was just something awful and filled the whole school. The teacher was not to be outdone and dismissed the whole class—except Snuffy. The teacher locked Snuffy in the school and let the rest of the kids go home. I never heard how long he kept Snuffy locked in, but I guess it was long enough to teach him the folly of trying this stunt again.

I found the Doukhobours to be good people, and we got along well. Ron Roylance had grown up in that country and could talk their brand of English about as well as they could. Some of his stories, told in the dialect, would have our whole camp rolling with laughter.

The economy of Midway-Greenwood depended on the lumber industry, particularly Boundary Sawmills, owned by John Sherbinnin. John was a big, happy-looking Doukhobour fellow who ran a million-dollar operation but didn't seem to let it worry him. I guess bureaucratic intrusion and government regulations were not as frustrating as they are today. His wife was pleasant and a gracious hostess. I was at their place a time or two. They had one daughter, Tanya, who was about eighteen. She was trim, attractive, and smart; in short, she was a really classy woman. She made it clear that she had a boyfriend at the University of B.C., but we went out a time or two anyway. I could have settled into a serious relationship with that girl. Too bad I didn't, as with her father's money I would not have had to worry about financing myself through medical training. Unfortunately, I heard that after John died both Tanya and her mother became hopeless alcoholics—too much money and not enough to do with it.

I also had a passing fling with a cute little student nurse from Greenwood; I met up with her again when I was an intern and she was nursing at the Jubilee Hospital in Victoria. She married an ex-TB patient from the hospital and, I believe, later divorced him.

We pretty well finished up the trans-provincial job. One of my last little chores there was to take my crew and a transit over and stake out the new route going down the hill into Grand Forks. I had the field notes and scale maps from the preliminary survey to follow, but it was the first piece of work that I was doing on my own. It made me consider switching from medicine to civil engineering when I went back to U of A.

# SIX

# University of Alberta Medical School

Back to the books again, our class was all gung-ho as this was our first year in the Faculty of Medicine and we were now on our way to becoming real doctors. In the back of my mind I knew I was aiming for surgery eventually. We still had some lectures in the pre-clinical sciences, but things were beginning to show a practical application. We had clinics on real live patients and learned to recognize what we heard when we listened through our stethoscopes and what a tumour felt like.

We broke up into groups and learned how to carry out different kinds of examinations, like rectal exams. The first one in our group was a Chinese girl named Amy Fong. By the time it was my turn to do the examination, Amy had already had a go at the "patient," and we usually just about had to drag the patient down off the chandelier after she got finished with him. The Dean of Medicine gave a lecture a short time later on being gentle when doing physical examinations. He told us that nothing gained the enmity of a patient like a "Rough Rectal."

Our class used to bus out to Fort Saskatchewan, north of Edmonton, for psychiatry clinics once a week. We conned the driver into stopping at a little pub just short of the mental hospital on our way out so we could pop in for a quick beer before we got to "the squirrel cage" for the afternoon clinic. I am sure some of those old chronic "alkies" could smell us the minute we stepped in the door. We thought it would develop more empathy in us before we interviewed those patients.

## Our Own Private Stiff

The anatomy lab, euphemistically referred to as the "stiff lab," was also an effective attention-getter for us first-year novices. We were broken up into groups of four, and each group was assigned to a table with our own private stiff (cadaver) on it. Thank God Fong was not with us.

After a lecture by the professor at eight in the morning, we spent until noon in the lab, methodically dissecting the structures that he had lectured on. The cadavers were all embalmed and were supposed to be nameless; however, we found out that our stiff was a Cree who had hung himself. The rope mark was clearly visible around his neck. We called him "Hung-by-the-Neck."

One thing in the stiff lab that we had to get used to was the smell of embalming fluid. The stuff they used ran pretty heavy to the Formalin and was effective, I guess, but would never replace Chanel No. 5 for aesthetic quality.

By this year I was involved in quite a few campus activities: some evening classes; the Outdoor Club, the Rifle Club, and the Boxing Club; and a job as night librarian at the Medical Library. To save the long hike back and forth from University Avenue, I got accepted into St. Stephen's College for room and board. The college was operated by the United Church and offered theology courses, but it had more room than necessary, so some students from other faculties boarded there and were charged a nominal sum for single or double room and board. St. Steve's was kitty-corner to the Medical Building and had a lot going on, including perennial bridge games, but if you really wanted to study you could go to your room and do so.

I further guaranteed the studying bit by working as night medical librarian. I was never bothered much on that job, only occasionally having to find someone a book. Mainly I opened up the doors at 7 p.m. and locked up at 10 p.m. Monday to Friday. I got lots of work done and earned a little money, and I continued that job for the rest of my university days.

Ernie "Tic" McCoy, a med student from Victoria, B.C., put me onto the library job as well as the deal with Weiler and Williams livestock brokers. "Tic" became a professor of pediatrics at U of A after he graduated and got into practice.

## Booby Traps and Bats

There were lots of pranks going on in St. Steve's, and there was always great rivalry between the med students and the engineers. One night a couple of engineers rigged up a booby trap on my room when I was at a party. They jimmied the lock on my door and ran a line from a light socket to the door lock. When I held the doorknob with one hand and inserted the key with the other, I completed the circuit and was supposed to get a good jolt from the 110-volt line. I did get a little zap alright, but not bad.

We got even with one of those engineers by climbing up in the belfry of St. Steve's and catching one of the hundreds of bats living there. We put it halfway down the inside of his jacket sleeve when he was in the dining room. When he came out and put his hand into his sleeve, the little monster hooked onto his bare skin with its claws and would not let go. There was a very entertaining song and dance performed while he was jumping around trying to get his arm out of his jacket.

Every spring in February the engineering students held the Engineers' Ball and Parade. Their theme song went:

Godiva was a lady who thru Coventry did ride
Showing to all the villagers her beautiful lily-white hide
The most observant man, an engineer of course,
Was the only man that noticed that Godiva rode a horse.

They managed to acquire a pure white horse, and one of their number, masquerading with long blonde curls and a suit of long white winter underwear, was to lead the parade.

A half dozen of us medical students happened to be lounging around the Med Building when we noticed that they had left their horse across the street, unattended except for one man while they ran inside St. Joseph's College to get their rider's costume in place. What an opportunity!

We casually but quickly strolled over, and after taking out the guard we made off with their horse. I was the best rider, so I jumped on this old nag and took off. The crowd of engineering students suddenly realized what was happening and I found myself with 300 howling engineers raging after me. I kicked that old horse in the ribs and had him going all out: across St. Steve's field and garden and through the Mewburn Pavilion parking lot, jumping any obstacles in the way. I finally lost the horde in back alleys behind 83 Avenue. My fellow horse thieves and I later rendezvoused for photographs with MED painted on the horse before returning him long after the parade was over and the crowd cleared. The pictures appeared in the *Edmonton Journal* and the meds chalked one up on the engineers.

## The Gadgeteer

We finished first year and were into second year when timing problems threw a hitch into my summer job and financial affairs. When the university session ended, everyone got out for the summer except the med students and a few civil engineers that had survey school. On account of the demand for medical officers in the war, the medical program was accelerated, with a longer session and consequently a shorter summer vacation.

I had no money left and I knew I could never save enough for the next year with only a short summer job. I was a little desperate and didn't

*Al Holley and his fellow medical students steal the lead horse of the Engineers' Parade and gain notoriety as horse thieves in the* Edmonton Journal. *Al and his friends pose proudly after escaping the posse of engineers: from left to right, Gordon Russell, Ira Young, Andy Adrekson, Al Holley, a passer-by from the Commerce Department, Mel Kreutz and Don Downie.*

know where to turn. Then I recalled seeing a notice for a research fellowship available for students at the end of second-year medicine, after they finished their clinical sciences and before they started straight clinical medicine. The Alberta College of Physicians and Surgeons offered the fellowship to stimulate research in basic science. I checked with the Dean's office and found that it had not yet been awarded, so I applied for the fellowship and got it. I went to see the professor of physiology and said that if it was agreeable to him and the committee, I would do the research work in his department and study the neurophysiology of neuromuscular motor end plates (myoneural junctions) in live animal muscles. Dr. Ardrey Downs said he would welcome me in his department. He was a graduate of the University of Pennsylvania in Philadelphia and was the personification of a gentleman and a scholar in every way.

The fellowship involved a year of research, at the end of which I would submit my thesis and be eligible for a Master of Science (M.Sc.) degree in neurophysiological research. The fellowship was worth $1,200—and I had to buy any special material from that award. The department of physiology supplied me with laboratory animals (rabbits) and routine staining materials, reagents, use of microscope, etc.

I was left pretty much on my own, but I would have welcomed some supervision. I read widely, covering everything that I could find in the medical library, but what I was doing was mostly original work, with not much already published on it. I learned to anaesthetize rabbits with open drop ether when taking muscle samples. I had to learn staining techniques and how to prepare slides and use a microscope. One of the popular tissue-stains for nerve tissue was Ranvier's gold chloride. I never did find out who Ranvier was. Another method using gold was that of Ramon Y Cajal, a Spaniard, I presumed. Another method involved using the Schiff reagent, which showed up nerve fibres very well.

We had a lab assistant, Charlie Heath, who was very hot on microphotography and had a good German Leica camera that could be fitted to a microscope. Charlie showed me quite a bit about photography, and we got a lot of good microphotographs.

Professor Downs, who was elderly, retired at the end of December and we got a new professor and head of the department, who was a real gadgeteer. They got him from the University of Manitoba in Winnipeg. He was not the man that Professor Downs was. This new department head's pet project was the electrogastrograph machine he developed, and which quickly became obsolete with the advent of fibreoptics and the gastroscope. The new head was only interested in his gadgets and didn't care a damn about anything else in his department. He never even so much as looked at what I was doing. I know my work was not worth much, but the other researchers and I were doing work in his department, so he should have given us some consideration and, especially for novices like me, some guidance. Professor William Stewart, a pharmacologist in the department, helped me with ideas quite often. Given some more time, and under his guidance, I think we could have produced quite a bit more.

Anyhow, the year passed and I presented my thesis, complete with original sketches, microphotographs, measurements, and what conclusions there were to be made. I never bothered to say goodbye to that department head and didn't bother to turn up at convocation to get my Master's degree. I got it in absentia.

I finished the project as soon as I could in order to get at summer work. Needless to say, I didn't have any of the $1,200 left at the end. I hitchhiked home to Trail and got work on the Fruitvale Highway Cut-off between Trail on the Columbia River and Salmo on the way to Nelson. It was a short summer and I was short of money. My mother didn't have much, but she loaned me $640. That was enough to keep me in medical school.

## Seagrams 83 Jig

For third year I rented a basement apartment with cooking facilities, close to the university, and really hit the books. My grocery bill was not very high. The place where I stayed, with Alan and Lillian Nicholls, was interesting. Lillian's brother was the bush pilot Max Ward, who I met occasionally and greatly admired. He was just getting his little charter service going out of Yellowknife. He had crashed his one and only plane when I lived there and was busy trying to finance another one; his insurance evidently was not too bountiful. Max persisted; he kept flying and eventually expanded to start up Wardair charter service, which became very successful. He eventually amalgamated with Canadian Pacific Airlines.

That year, as well as working as a proofreader on the editorial staff of the university yearbook, I was president of the Outdoor Club. We had a cabin down on the riverbank and held work parties on weekends to develop the place. We used to buy twelve dozen cartons of honey-dipped doughnuts and keep them frozen in the cabin during the winter. I had a key to the cabin, so on the nights when I did not have much food in my cupboard, I had warmed-up doughnuts and coffee at the cabin for supper. They filled me up so I could go back to work anyway.

Med III was interesting, as a lot of it was in the teaching hospitals, even though it often meant stirring around to catch a cold winter streetcar to the other side of the city for a seven o'clock lecture or clinic.

I fell in love with several different women during that year. Settling down in a cozy nest in the west was not on my program, so with these situations we phased in and phased out again. I had a lot of surgery to learn when I finished medical school and had a lot of travelling to do to find what I needed to learn.

One date I went on I didn't forget easily. I was invited to the University Hospital nurses' graduation dinner and dance in the Macdonald Hotel ballroom. My date was on the executive of the graduating class. On this account we were seated directly in front of the head table. Thinking that the speeches might be long I put a mickey of rye and Seven-Up in my suitcoat breast pocket.

The dinner was over, and before the presentations the M.C. announced that we would be favoured with an interlude of piano music by one of the talented nurses. She was playing a selection from Debussy's "Claire de Lune" and was just at a very soft and quiet part of the piece when—Bam!! An explosion like a twelve-gauge shotgun rocked the room. Everyone looked around, startled, wondering what had happened.

Just then I felt something warm and wet trickling down the side of my shirt. I carefully put my hand into my inside jacket pocket and pricked my finger on a glass splinter from my shattered mickey. The girl on the left side of me slid her table napkin over to me and I carefully stuffed it inside my jacket to soak up some of the booze trickling down. The girl on the right side of me did the same, until I pretty well got it soaked up.

Meanwhile, the old director of nursing and the hospital superintendent and other dignitaries were all surveying the crowd like a corvette captain glassing the water for signs of a periscope. I looked around me like everyone else, maintaining a serene and smiling countenance in spite of the fact that my left side was getting wet all the way down to my crotch. Everyone at my table maintained an air of the greatest innocence, although they were all just about busting a gut trying to keep straight faces.

During intermission in the men's room I was able to get some towels to sponge myself dry, sort of. All the guys were asking, "What the hell was that great bang up there?" I remained silent on the issue, but it was hard to dance a Strauss waltz with dignity while the skin of my balls was tingling from the astringent properties of a soak in Seagrams 83. I had a recurring urge to do a little jig.

In my ignorance I had added the carbonated mixer to the rye in a bottle with a screw top. What with the heat of the room and my body heat, it built up pressure until she blew. It sure made great conversation material, not only for our table, but also for the whole crowd.

## "Squawtalmaw" and "M'chimn'a"

During third year I went over to the Charles Camsell Indian Hospital in Edmonton and met Dr. Lyn Falconer, director of Indian Health Services, and lined up a job for Western Canada for the summer. I would go out to all the reservations and settlements in Alberta, doing travelling clinics with the X-ray technicians and public health nurses. I would also drive the van if needed, reload X-ray cassettes in the darkroom tent, and assist whomever needed help.

The job started and finished at Edmonton, so I did not have to concern myself with transportation to the job. At the end of Med III I reported to Dr. Falconer at the Camsell Hospital and for a couple of weeks worked on the wards, sat in with Dr. Tom Orford reading chest X-rays, attended conferences, and learned a lot about tuberculosis and Native and Inuit patients.

We went on our first travelling clinic to Northern Alberta and the Lac la Biche area. I worked mainly as X-ray assistant here. Then Don Harkness, the crew, and I travelled to the Blackfoot reserve at Gleichen and to the Blood reserve near Cardston in Southern Alberta—Mormon country. Here we met Chief Charlie Shot-on-both-Sides. The old chief spoke good English and told us interesting stories about Indian and cowboy life in early Alberta.

Later in the summer there was supposed to be a big powwow and Sun Dance in the foothills west of Rocky Mountain House. The Sun Child Crees were supposed to attend; they had never had any medical attention or

*The Cree at Rocky Mountain House set up the Sun Dance Lodge for the powwow.*

much contact with white men and were one of the tribes that had never signed a treaty with the Canadian government. Veteran Indian Health nurse Rita Murphy and I were delegated to attend this social gathering. Our job was to look after any and all minor ailments and to develop some rapport with these Natives, but not to even mention immunization or chest X-rays for tuberculosis, and especially not to talk about admitting anyone to hospital for tuberculosis treatment. The Native bands said that their people went to the white man's hospital, died there, and never came back. That wasn't too far wrong at that time, but we hoped to develop some treatment that would cure them and get them back home fairly soon.

This was a P.R. trip. Rita and I booked in at the one hotel available in Rocky Mountain House, and the next day we followed the Indian agent from Rocky Mountain House on a trail out past Kootenai Flats to a secluded spot in the foothills. The Native bands had their tents set up in a big circle about a half mile in diameter.

In the centre they were setting up the Sun Dance lodge. Smaller trees were leaned in a circle around a big poplar tree to make a sort of big tepee. Then, about four feet from the inside wall, a low wall of poplar brush stood. The dancers performed inside this little circle. At a break in this wall but still inside the main wall of the lodge there was a small campfire within a circle of rocks, and here, wreathed in smoke, sat the drummers beating their tom-toms. I think they warmed their drums at the fire once in awhile to improve the tone.

We borrowed a tent and an axe and Rita and I set up our medical tent in the big circle along with the rest of them. In the tent we kept a good supply of throat lozenges, ASA, 222s and 292s, and elastic bandages for minor injuries or afflictions that might occur during the three-day Sun Dance. There were Native people from all over Alberta and Saskatchewan and from Montana in the U.S. All day and all night the tom-toms beat and the dancers stamped. At the same time a whole cavalcade of men and boys rode their horses around and round within the circle of tents, chanting and singing. The Sun Dance is a traditional ceremony of the Plains Indians and is not normally seen in northern or B.C. tribes.

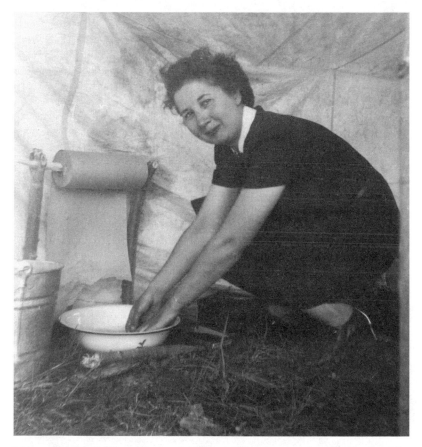

*Nurse Rita Murphy scrubs up in our medical tent at the Sun Dance. The "Holley patented towel roller" is in the background.*

*Doc Holley welcomes patients to his new medical tent during his P.R. trip to Rocky Mountain House.*

Rita and I circulated, chatting with the people and doing a little first aid when asked, just making our presence known, finding out some attitudes.

I recall talking to Jim Strawberry, a member of the Sun Child band on the Big Horn River. He asked about one of their people in hospital in Calgary. I found out what I could for him and later sought him out and told him what I had learned from the Indian agent. It was not good. I could not help noticing the pale appearance of Jim's teenage son. Both Rita and I noticed it and both had the same idea—here was a boy who had advanced active tuberculosis and should be quickly removed from his community to stop him from spitting and coughing TB bugs in every direction. That was not what we were there for, so we kept quiet for now. A lot of patient education was going to be necessary; we wouldn't push things on our first encounter.

We got a pretty good impression of the general health of those Natives to report to the consultants in the division when we returned to Edmonton. We also got some good pictures.

After we got back from that trip, I was soon bouncing over the muskeg to Fort McMurray on the Northern Alberta Railway. There we met the Indian Affairs treaty party and travelled by boat down the Athabasca River to Fort Chipewyan at the west end of Lake Athabasca. The first night out we pulled into shore at suppertime and tied up the boat while we cooked some food.

On the riverbank there were tar sand outcroppings everywhere. When we got a good fire going we put some chunks of this stuff on the coals and it smouldered away with lots of smoke. In a short while our camp was completely deserted by the hordes of mosquitoes that surrounded us when we first came ashore. After supper we decided to spend the night there since it was so free from mosquitoes. We banked up the fire, taking care to pile a goodly amount of tar sand all around to keep our smudge going all night. We rolled up in our sleeping bags and slept until daylight. After a quick breakfast of bacon and eggs we pushed off down the river.

Travelling on the Athabasca was a daylight proposition as there were many sandbars. The bowman sat up front with a long pole for pushing us off the bars and from his vantage point signalled the skipper which way to go to keep in the channel. Embarras Portage was particularly tricky. The big freight barges had to wait for high water before attempting to pass through. This area was a popular place for the band to trap muskrats. Countless waterfowl and muskrats inhabited thousands of acres of flooded marshland. A short time after we passed Embarras we came out on Lake Athabasca. Across the lake, on the northwest end, was Fort Chipewyan. We tied up at the wharf there where the freight barges used to load.

The next day the Treaty Party took place. The Indian agent and his assistant, accompanied by two RCMP in scarlet tunics and all spit and polish, set up a table and chairs. They gave out $5 to each man, woman, and child listed in their treaty book for that band. The procedure was made a very solemn occasion. While that was being done, Martin Goodall, the X-ray tech, and I cranked up the gas-powered generator and did chest X-rays on all the people.

Martin told me that to do an X-ray survey on those Chipewyans you only needed to know two words in their language: "Squawtalmaw," which meant "breathe in," and then when you got your picture it was "M'chimn'a," which meant "breathe away." He said the last words were not so important as they always started breathing again sooner or later.

## Dental Hero, Terror of Abscesses Everywhere

I had spent time in the hospital dental clinic in Edmonton, learning how to do proper nerve blocks and how to use dental instruments to do extractions. An aching tooth was something that Native people as well as others in the back country do not tolerate well. They might be dying of advanced tuberculosis and could accept that, but I have seen trappers travel 200 to 300 miles by canoe or dog team to get an aching tooth pulled. Extraction was the best we could offer. Fillings, crown, root canals, and the like were for city dwellers.

On July 1, 1950, we were in Fort Chipewyan when someone came along to report that a woman in the settlement had a badly abscessed and aching tooth. Here was my chance to be a hero—there was no one else to do it. I gathered up the dental kit and followed the messenger up the hill to the woman's cabin. She was a big, very fat Chipewyan woman who spoke good English. She had a hell of an abscess in the lower first molar on the right. I knew that in the face of her active abscess the local anaesthetic likely wouldn't work very well, but I did the best I could and warned her that it might not be too good. I guess it hurt so bad that she would put up with some extra pain just to get rid of the damned thing. I checked over the instruments and picked out a forceps that I thought would do.

I remembered what the dentist told me: for incisors and any other tooth with a single root you use a smaller forceps and twist while you pull to screw the tooth out of the socket. For molars, which have two, three, or four roots, you should use a large forceps and rock the tooth back and forth while you pull and hope you can rock it right out.

I picked out a big sturdy forceps and got a mouth gag to hold her jaws open. I had her in a chair in the middle of the room, ready to go.

The patient said to me, "If it hurts, can I squeeze your leg?"

I got a good grip on the molar and I said, "Squeeze away." She had a grip on my right thigh with both hands. I rocked and pulled while she squeezed. Eventually the tooth came out, complete with all its roots. I gave her a wad of cotton to chomp down on to stop the bleeding. If I'd had a bottle of whisky I would have gladly shared it with her.

Flushed with success from my first big case, I eventually pulled quite a few bad teeth at such places as Fond du Lac, Stony Rapids, and other ports of call.

When we were finished at Stony Rapids, we returned back down the lake to Fort Chipewyan. The day before we left Stony Rapids we had the best Arctic grayling fishing I have ever seen. We used a flat-bottomed boat with a ten-horse kicker on it, ran up the mouth of the river to where it emptied into the lake in about ten feet of water, threw an old car motor overboard for an anchor, then cast spinners in every direction. In short order we had a dozen grayling averaging two or three pounds each.

Stony Rapids is at the east end of Lake Athabasca, just inside the Alberta-Saskatchewan border. There was little access to it at that time, but I imagine you can now reach it by road from Prince Albert. To the north it is quite close to the Northwest Territories. I would like to get up there again.

As soon as we got reorganized we left the lake and headed up to Riviere des Roches en route to Fort Fitzgerald and Fort Smith. From Riviere des Roches we entered the Peace River, which by now was a pretty good size.

There is a fourteen-mile portage between Fitzgerald and Fort Smith due to a very rough and rocky stretch of river. Over this portage, two identical stretches of road run side by side, one built by the Hudson's Bay Company and the other by their opposition, the Northern Transportation Co. One would suspect that the two outfits didn't get along. Both the HBC and the NT Co. ran riverboats and freight barges from Fort McMurray and Waterways, Alberta, down the Athabasca, across the end of the lake at Fort Chip, down Riviere des Roches, up the Peace, and down the Slave into Great Slave Lake. They finally entered the Mackenzie River at Fort Providence and ran this river to Inuvik and Aklavik, where the Mackenzie empties into the Arctic Ocean.

Fort Smith is on the Slave River, which empties into Great Slave Lake, and was at that time the capital and administration centre of the Northwest Territories. Now Yellowknife has that honour. Fort Smith had a taxi service, a jail, government offices, bootlegger, whorehouse, and I don't know what other services befitting an important metropolis.

The taxi driver was a little weasel of a man. His wife was a big woman, weighing about 200 pounds. This taxi driver got thrown in the Crowbar

Hotel for drunken driving. His wife went down to the jail and said she wanted to talk to her husband. They let her in, and a few minutes later they heard this great commotion, with slam-banging coming from his cell. They ran in to see what was going on and found his big wife just beating the hell out of her husband, the taxi man, for getting drunk on the job.

We did chest X-rays on everybody we could catch up to in Fitzgerald and Smith, crossed Great Slave Lake to Yellowknife, then flew back to Edmonton in a DC3. That ended a good summer job.

## Lady Wrestler

We were now about to enter our fourth and final year of medical school, six years since we started pre-med. By now we had learned enough to realize how much more there was to learn and how pitifully little we really knew. I was going to go back into St. Steve's this year, but one of my buddies told me over coffee one day of a great place to stay, at a cheap cost and with great food, over on Saskatchewan Drive, not too far away. I walked over to check it out.

A slightly mousy but not unattractive woman and her husband had an extra room and would give me room and board, so I moved in. This woman just stripped her gears to put out good meals. I used to try to show my appreciation for the good food, but her miserable, morose, son-of-a-bitch of a husband would never say anything nice about the food or about her or anything else, for that matter.

He had a gunsmith shop in the basement where he spent quite a bit of time. He and I maintained a sort of cordial disregard. Anytime that he was away and I was up studying in my room, she came up and was all over me like a lady wrestler. She seemed to just crave affection, and knowing her husband, I could see why.

About two weeks after I moved in I was feeling a little cruddy, so stayed home in bed. My landlady came up to see me. Next thing I knew she was snuggled up in bed with me. With all due apologies for being a poor sport and all, I quickly got up and got dressed—I had visions of being on the wrong end of one of the old Colt .45s that her dear husband was shining up in his shop.

Later that afternoon I crawled into bed again for a short nap. She repeated the performance. I jumped out of bed, and while I was getting dressed I explained to her that I thought she was real nice and all, but that I didn't want to get my head blown off by her miserable husband. I paid my board bill up to date and moved back into St. Steve's. She was a nice lady, but I couldn't keep her out of bed—my bed.

## How to Do a Schottische

When the session got under way we found out that the teaching hospitals were taking a limited number of clinical clerks from fourth-year medicine. My friend Don, one of the female students, and I were accepted into the Royal Alexandria Hospital. In return for doing the case histories and physical exams on all the new admissions, we got our room and board at the hospital. This was a great deal. We stayed in the interns' residence and averaged about three to four hours' work per day, long enough to do a complete work-up on three new patients each day and complete their histories. A senior intern or a resident usually checked our case histories and results with us and discussed a proposed plan of treatment; this was further checked over by a consultant on staff before the plan was implemented.

Working as a clinical clerk was almost like being a junior intern, except that we spent more time writing case histories and not so much of the day working in the hospital wards. Nor did we get a chance to work with the surgeons in the OR (operating room).

The Royal Alex, as it was affectionately called, was a good teaching hospital and a good place to learn. Most of the staff were on the university teaching staff, but were usually a bit more informal than the full-timers at the University Hospital. We had ample time for studying; in fact, we had to keep our marks high in order to stay on the program.

And the student nurses at the Alex were just the sweetest dolls you could imagine. My girlfriend and I became famous after a staff barn dance when she fell on me and broke my rib. We were showing the others how to do a schottische when we slipped on the floor and landed with her elbow in my ribs. That night I didn't feel it so much, probably because we were somewhat anaesthetized. The next morning, though, it hurt so badly that I got it X-rayed.

Everybody thought it was funny except me. The gossip around the interns' and the nurses' quarters was, "Did you hear about Al Holley? His girlfriend fell on him and broke his ribs. Ho! Ho! Ho! She wasn't all that big, either." My cracked rib was sore for a month.

Final exams are a terrible experience at the best of times, especially the orals, but we all seemed to struggle through them and none of our class jumped off the High Level Bridge.

When I finished my last exam I made arrangements to get my chronically infected tonsils out. I had been plagued with tonsil infections over the past couple of years and swore that the minute I finished exams I would get rid of those things. The hospital would take me without charge since I had worked there all year. The surgical boys told me that the man to get was Dr. Jack Lees, a general surgeon who did the slickest T&A

69

(tonsillectomy and adenoidectomy) at the Royal Alex, way better than any of the ENT (ear, nose, and throat) specialists. He agreed, and I was duly booked. Most of the nursing staff, especially the students, seemed to think this was some sort of festive occasion, so when I was shown my bed the night before surgery, the sheets had been apple-pied by the afternoon shift. There was no way I could get into that damned bed. I had to take all the bedclothes off and make it over.

I shared a two-bed ward with a Ukrainian fellow. About eleven o'clock that night, after everything was quiet, my very attractive girlfriend, who was senior nurse on the ward, came tippy-toeing in to say "good night." She hauled over a set of screens and placed them all around my bed, squeezed inside, turned back the sheets, and jumped in, leaving her co-worker to stand guard. Oh, how sweet life can be!

A half-hour later the screens were put back in their place against the wall and my sweetie returned to work. My Ukrainian roommate, who we thought was sleeping, stirred around in bed and said to me, "That noisse, she is some kind you goil friend?"

I said, "Yeah, some kind," and went peacefully to sleep.

SEVEN

# Bush Intern

I had two months before I reported to the Jubilee Hospital in Victoria for my junior internship, and Indian Health Services had a two-month junket lined up that was just the ticket. Two senior field nurses, Amy Wilson and Eileen Bond; X-ray technician George Berg; and a medical officer (me) would start at Dawson Creek, B.C., Mile Zero of the Alaska Highway, in two vehicles and would cover every Indian settlement from Dawson Creek to the Alaska border. We had two months to complete our trip. Dr. J.P. Harvey and nurse Agnes Whittaker would also assist us on the first leg of our trip, from Dawson Creek to Fort Nelson. I would change X-ray cassettes in the darkroom tent for George and help him however I could, work with the field nurses where indicated, act as a medical officer, and pull aching teeth. Furthermore, I would drive our old Dodge Carryall that hauled the gas-powered generator and portable X-ray machine. On the first of May we headed up the road to Dawson Creek.

The nurses were old hands at this sort of safari. They had a new Ford pickup and could make better time than we could, but we kept in touch along the way. George was an easygoing guy who had worked at the hospital in Dawson City in the Yukon in his earlier days.

We checked in with the Indian agent whenever we were in an area where there was one. Travelling up the Alaska (Alcan) Highway we found that we could travel 50 to 60 miles per hour on the gravel with no problems. If we pushed it past that speed we started popping tires. So we didn't rush.

We saw our first patients at Blueberry, 20 to 30 miles off the highway, northeast of Fort St. John. We had a great load of X-ray film in the old Dodge, which made it ride pretty fair. We lost a few days when we bent a drive shaft and had to wait for them to fly one up from Edmonton. Having

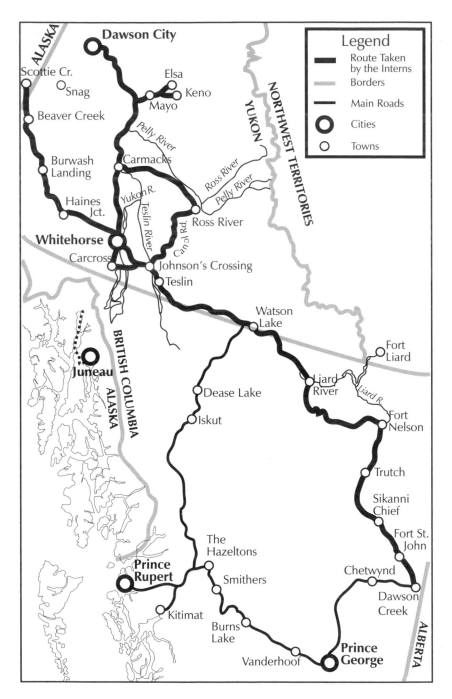

*Al, Miss Whittaker and George Berg pose at Mile Zero in Dawson Creek, B.C., the starting point of their summer trek across the North.*

got that replaced we headed up the highway again, past Beaton River, Sikanni Chief, and Trutch to Fort Nelson, which was quite a place at that time. The economy was based on the Air Force station, oil and gas exploration, trapping, a little logging, and rough-and-tumble motels and cafes serving the traffic on the Alaska Highway.

The diminutive Indian agent in Fort Nelson, "Petit Joe" Galibois, showed us one whole street where the couples were all shack-ups, there was not one married couple on the whole street, according to him. With

*On the first leg of our tour, "Petit Joe" Galabois, Miss Whittaker, Dr. Harvey and I cross the Fort Nelson River in this riverboat (top left). Afterwards, we visited Liard Hot Springs (bottom left) and then met this man at our clinic in Teslin (right).*

Petit Joe, we loaded our stuff and ourselves on a riverboat and crossed the Fort Nelson River to the village on the other side; the residents were either Sikanni or Beaver, intermarried.

We X-rayed and inoculated everybody we could catch, made it back across the fast-flowing Fort Nelson River and back on the road. Our next stop was Steamboat Mountain, then Liard Hot Springs, where George and I had a nice soothing bath. The Hot Springs were barely developed, but there was a trail hacked out through the ferns and tropical vegetation to the springs, where the warm water seeped down the side of the valley all year long. In a big pool, about a hundred feet across, the water was 100 degrees F, and in a smaller bowl, where the water came out through the rocks, it was about 120 degrees—you had to get in carefully, one foot at a time, and we didn't stay there long. An old-timer came along and scooped a drinking glassful out of the small hot pool where we were soaking our tired feet. He said that sulphur water had great medicinal value. We didn't know whether the benefits would come from the sulphur water or our sweaty feet—they both smelled about the same.

Now, 40 years later, there is a motel at Liard, the springs are somewhat developed, there is a campground, and it is a tourist "stop of interest."

We passed Lower Post on the Liard River, then came to Watson Lake, YT, where the U.S. Air Force base and airstrip were located—part of the northwest staging route used by American Air Force planes en route to Alaska. There was a motel at Watson Lake, built from army construction huts, where we booked in. Watson Lake also had a bar, patronized by highway maintenance crews and the few early adventurous tourists.

I recall rescuing a terrified Doberman pinscher from a bunch of malamutes in the yard in front of the motel. This young dog ran right between my legs and wouldn't budge. I chased the malamutes away; otherwise they would have torn it to pieces. The Doberman followed us into our unit and wouldn't leave us. I took it outside so it could go to the bathroom at bedtime, and it came right back in and curled up in the corner for the night. Before we left in the morning I delivered it to the man at the bar, who said he would look after it.

Our next stop was Teslin, on the lake of the same name. Teslin was once on the water route to Lac Laberge and the Klondike. The Native people here are famous for the snowshoes they make. I bought a pair to take home. We X-rayed all the people at Teslin, who belonged to the T'lingit tribe. They were a friendly bunch.

We finally arrived at Whitehorse. Even in 1950 Whitehorse was a thriving little city, located on the Yukon River, with the resultant riverboat traffic in the summer. Whitehorse was also the terminus of the Yukon and White Pass Railway, running from Skagway to Whitehorse. There was a large and quite active American Air Force base; it was an important stopping place on the Alaska Highway. Dawson City was still the capital of the Yukon Territory, a holdover from gold-rush days, but Whitehorse was already assuming the role of primary importance and was recognized as the distributing centre, communications centre, and generally the gateway from the Yukon to the outside world.

In the Yukon, as in the Northwest Territories, if you were going to Edmonton or Vancouver or such places, you were said to be "going out." I can only assume that when you were in Whitehorse or Dawson City you were considered to be "in."

After a few days in Whitehorse we travelled to Haines Junction, southwest of Whitehorse, where a road branched off the Alaska Highway and went south to the coast at Anchorage, Alaska. We X-rayed Native people here and at Aishihik, where there was a fair number. From Haines we proceeded to Burwash Landing, not so far from Mount Logan and Mount St. Elias.

We also visited Snag, a highway camp where the coldest temperature in the North American continent was recorded, -83 degrees F. The

*Old Man Lewis ran the Burwash Bar, where we happily drank his HBC rum and moonshine.*

workmen at Snag told us that when they walked outside in that weather their breath crackled as it froze when it was drifting past their ears.

At Burwash Landing we were at the end of beautiful Kluane Lake. At Burwash's bar you could get a drink of HBC overproof rum, whisky, or moonshine. In that area there was also a good number of white Dahl sheep, a trophy treasured by all big-game hunters. Burwash had great country with scenery that would almost take your breath away.

## Round-up

While we were in that area we heard about a group of Natives who had been eluding white attempts to X-ray and vaccinate them. They were presently camped just across the border at Scottie Creek, Alaska. It was important to get this group of people immunized because they lived close to the highway—infectious diseases spread faster and farther when people live near main roads.

We left early one morning for Scottie Creek and drove in on their camp before they were even wide-awake. The two nurses rounded them all up, while George and I cranked up the generator and the portable X-ray. We nailed an X-ray cassette holder up between two poplar trees and we were in business.

I quickly set up the darkroom tent while George was getting the first people X-rayed, and I could soon give George a continuous supply of fresh films after packaging the exposed stuff. Amy and Eileen got their equipment set up and vaccinated for small pox and inoculated for diphtheria before these people knew what was going on.

The immunizations that the nurses were doing were quite effective, so once they were done, these people were relatively safe from the two worst highly infectious diseases. Dr. Orford and Dr. Matas at the Camsell Hospital would read all the TB X-rays when we got them back. Those patients that showed active TB would have to be tracked down and brought in for treatment. I kind of wished I was going to be around for that, as catching up to them in that wild country would be an interesting challenge.

After crossing the Alaska border to see the Scottie Creek bunch, we thought we had better get back in our own territory, so headed back to Whitehorse. We loafed around there for a couple of days; made a trip to Carcross on Lake Bennett, on the route of the gold seekers to the Klondike; visited Atlin, which is one of the most scenic places I have seen; and then went back to Whitehorse.

While staying in a motel there, George and I had a very exhilarating swim in the pool. The sign said "heated pool," so we dived in. Wow! It was cold! I am not a great swimmer, but I got to the opposite side of the pool barely touching the water on the way. The pool was excavated out of the permafrost and the hotel had turned the heat off the day before. It sure sharpened us up for the rest of the day.

## Bush Gymnastics

We gathered up a supply of food and assorted camping supplies for our next safari up the abandoned Canol pipeline road from Johnson's Crossing on the Alaska Highway to Ross River. The pipeline was built during World War II to pipe oil from Norman Wells to a refinery at Whitehorse for military use if necessary. The line was now abandoned and the road was in rough shape. In places we travelled down creekbeds, and I wondered if the old Dodge was going to hold together. Eileen and Amy stuck right with us in their Ford pickup.

At one bridge, part of the middle trestle had begun to collapse, but the decking was still holding together. It was about twenty feet to the creek below, not too bad. We got a bunch of spare planks and laid them end to end to reinforce the part that was sagging badly, then I jumped in and crawled the old Dodge across in low gear. The nurses followed us over. Once across we stopped for lunch. I got out my fishing rod and in a few minutes had five grayling, about three-quarters of a pound each. We fried them up right there and they were delicious (grayling are much like rainbow trout).

We pushed on up the road, passing a few deserted maintenance camps on the way. Shortly before suppertime we arrived at the Pelly River

*Canol Road had some dangerous spots in 1951. Everyone was out of the truck but me. After crossing I caught five grayling in this river.*

a little below where the Ross joins it. There was a small cable ferry we could use to cross the Pelly. The ferry consisted of planks laid on two pontoons, and the thing was framed up with more planks to give it some substance and stability—not a large craft. Passengers cranked a handle to pull the ferry across on the cable. Right now the ferry was pulled up with the pontoons resting on the gravel on the shore side; the outer ends of the pontoons were in the current.

George and I got a couple of poles and pried the contraption a little further into the river. There were a couple of planks to drive up on from the shore side. To get the shore-side pontoons off the gravel we figured I had to drive ahead far enough to tip the pontoons at the deep-water end down and lift the other end off the shore. We opened both windows in the Dodge, and with me alone in the cab I drove her up on the planks and far enough ahead to get her floating free. That done, I turned off the ignition, set the brakes, blocked the wheels, and we cranked ourselves across. Then we cranked the ferry back across and the intrepid nurses followed us over.

On the far (north) side of the Pelly River was a big flat with a couple of old log cabins on it. After exploring a bit to find a place to set up camp, we encountered an elderly woman setting traps for "gophers" (actually Columbia ground squirrels). They were like large gophers and were quite plentiful. She told us that the rest of her camp was about six miles farther ahead up in the mountains, fishing. They had left her behind as she was too crippled to keep up with them. She would trap gophers to eat until they got back.

We set up our camp and made supper and later rolled into our sleeping bags. In the morning when we were having coffee we heard an aircraft. A short time later Bud Harbottle of Yukon Airways walked into our camp. We gave him a cup of coffee. He said he saw our camp and vehicles from the air and dropped down on the river to see how we were doing. He agreed to drop a message for us at the fish camp, asking the people there to come down and see us.

The way the bush pilots dropped messages for people on the ground was to cram the message inside the core of a roll of toilet paper, then unravel a bit of tissue to get the roll spinning, and toss her overboard. As it spun while unwinding to the ground, a long tail of tissue floated out behind, making it easy to find the core with the message when it reached the ground. We thought this was a great idea and got the message ready for him.

*Miss Wilson consoles an 80-year-old woman at Ross River.*

We heard him revving up his motor and thought he was away. A half-hour later, however, he came walking back into camp with a look on his face that was hard to describe.

"Well," he said, "the plane is hanging on the ferry cable in the middle of the river!" He was trying to take off from upstream when he got windcocked and couldn't get enough power to turn his plane around and get away from the cable. An upstream wind kept his tail pointed upriver, and the swift current carried his pontoons and the plane downstream. Before he could get turned around, the windshield caught on the ferry cable, which was strung across the river eight or nine feet above the water. His left pontoon went under and the plane started to go down. Bud climbed out and grabbed the ferry cable, moving hand over hand from the middle of the river to shore. He dropped to the ground and walked to our camp.

Meantime the plane flipped around until the prop shaft caught on the cable, and that was how the plane was hanging. We were all in a bit of a bind. Bud had no more plane; we had no way of getting back out, as the plane was

*We camp out by a quiet lake on Canol Rd. Strips of moose meat hang on poles to dry in the sun.*

*Bud Hardbottle's plane floats upside-down in the Pelly River after hitting the ferry cable.*

hung up on our ferry cable in the middle of the river. There was a suspension footbridge over the river just above the crossing, and we could have travelled over that to get back the way we came, but it was a long way to walk back to the highway from Ross River. I didn't ask the old woman for her opinion of the situation, but I'm sure she must have found the whole thing interesting.

I don't remember, myself, trying to pray for some means of salvation, but somebody in the outfit must have said the right words. Our salvation came in the form of a huge flatdeck truck with a big Mack engine, owned by Reimer Trucking from Calgary. This outfit arrived at the south side of the river to start hauling abandoned oil pipe back out to the highway. We all jumped for joy at the sight, but I think Bud jumped the highest. He had performed quite a feat in coming hand over hand on the cable all the way from midriver, but he was a little upset at the thought of losing his aircraft as well as nullifying the prospects of any further traffic crossing on the ferry, including our vehicles.

The guys with the trucking outfit had lots of rigging with them, including rope and cable. While we drank coffee back at our camp, the salvation project began. Bud found a moosehide boat on the riverbank. In this cranky and somewhat unmanageable craft, he paddled out to the aircraft and secured a rope to the prop shaft. The trucker then tied a light cable to the end of the rope on the shore. Bud was able to haul this cable through the current out to the aircraft, where he attached it to the prop shaft. They then slowly dragged the aircraft up the cable with the truck's winch. When the aircraft got close to the shore and the uphill drag got pretty heavy, they attached a heavier cable to the winch to keep from losing the aircraft in the river. Once on shore, Bud and the mechanics removed the instrument panel and the pontoons from his plane—the items he wanted to salvage. He left the rest.

We forgot about any further attempts to round up the locals for the time being. We just wanted to get our outfit back across the river and get the hell out of there. We drove our rigs down to the riverbank and cranked ourselves back across without mishap. I was not too happy about trusting the ferry cable after we dragged the plane over it, but there wasn't much alternative. Anyway, we all got back over, leaving the old lady to tell the story to her people.

We made it over the rough road and back to Whitehorse, where we reported our adventurous but unprofitable trip to the Indian agent.

## Carmacks Town Brawl

We had two last visits to make—to Carmacks via Mayo Landing by road, then from Mayo to Dawson City by air, in a Canadian Air Force DC3. The drive from Whitehorse to Mayo was a slow dusty trip on what was built as a winter cat road with volcanic ash. The thick dust floated straight up and filled the gap in the jack pines from border to border, making it completely impossible to see behind us. Luckily we did not encounter any other vehicles all the way to Mayo. We put wet handkerchiefs over our mouths and noses to breathe through. Eileen and Amy pulled off and gave us a half-hour head start to let the dust settle.

At Mayo, the nurses slept in somebody's house and George and I flopped our bedrolls in the old poker parlour; no games were going on at the time. The next day our goal was the Native village at Carmacks, a few miles farther along the Yukon River. There was a vacant nursing station for us to stay in near the village.

We got there just at dusk, and our first spectacle was a man dragging a drunken, passed-out woman by the hair, pulling her off the truck trail so that we could get by. An interesting welcoming committee!

The river paddlewheelers used to stop at Carmacks to load cordwood for their boilers, and we guessed that these boats were the source of booze for the locals—besides homebrew.

We went on to the old nursing station, where we shooed out the mice and made ourselves comfortable for the night. The Indian agent and his clerk arrived at the village next morning, and they and the nurses went on a tour.

Carmacks was, by their description, a scene of absolute mayhem. One big man was chopping stovepipes down with his axe. Another lunged at one of the nurses, but three of the women tackled him and flattened him on the ground. As they were holding him down, one of the women

*After a big moonshine bust near the Carmacks Nursing Station in August 1951, the mayhem that greeted us on our arrival calmed down considerably.*

had her derriere sticking out in the breeze, and a passing malamute reached out and took a big bite.

One of the nurses got a picture, but her timing was just a bit too slow, the dog having just let go when she snapped her camera. In view of the goings on, and with information that they had a bunch of moonshine somewhere around, the Indian agent sent a message on the telegraph line upriver to the RCMP at Stewart.

A constable came up the river with a canoe and kicker and arrested some of the more wild people, who would appear in court at Dawson when court could be convened. Someone told the constable that they had a batch of brew in a cabin not far from the nurses' station. He came along to seize the brew and found a whole four-gallon pot. When he went to carry it out the door, several women blocked the doorway and wouldn't let him out with it. He came up to the cabin to see if someone could help him. The two nurses immediately volunteered my help, no doubt knowing that I had a way with women.

I went with him and kept the women back while the constable carried the pot over to our cabin. He poured a small portion into bottles that he could cork and transport in the canoe as exhibits for court. The brew looked like dishwater but had a rather pleasant aroma. I asked one of the locals what was in it.

He said, "Oh, some raisins and sugar and potato peelings and then you put it by the stove for a few days, then you throw in some those headache pills; when it goes chug! chug! you drink 'um."

I saved a small bottle to take back with me, jammed a cork in it, and threw it in my suitcase. The next time I opened my suitcase I found the cork blown out and all my clothes saturated and smelling like sweetish moonshine-flavoured potato peelings. What a mess!

After X-raying and immunizing all the people at the village, we drove back to Mayo, locked up our vehicles at the airstrip, and piled our gear, generator, and X-ray machine by the end of the runway for loading. An RCAF DC3 arrived shortly. We landed at a gravelled airstrip at Dawson

City and checked into the old Flora Dora Hotel. George, Amy, Eileen, and I toured Dawson City and environs, including the waterfront where the paddlewheelers docked and the Klondike River dredging operations were, and walked to Robert Service's cabin. There were few tourists at that time since the road from Whitehorse to Dawson was not open to traffic and a boat hadn't recently arrived.

The bar at the Flora Dora was licensed to serve beer and wine only, in the wisdom of the stupid bureaucrats "from the outside." However, if you asked for a rye and water, as we did, the bartender simply served you from a jug under the counter instead of from the beer taps on top of the counter. I didn't notice any more drunks there than anywhere else, probably less.

We finished all the work that we had to do. Amy and Eileen boarded a riverboat that would drop them off at Carmacks, where they would climb into their pickup truck for their long return trip home. George and I packed all our gear into the DC3 the next day and went back to Mayo. We transferred our stuff to the old Dodge and started on our own journey through the dust back to the highway. We stayed overnight in Whitehorse before heading back down the Alaska Highway that we had driven up two months ago. We missed the company of the two nurses, who were good travelling companions and asked for no favours while doing their share of whatever there was to do.

We had an interesting little sidelight in Whitehorse. We were in the Whitehorse Inn when George Berg saw an old acquaintance. George invited him to sit down for a drink and asked how he was doing. The fellow said he would be doing a lot better, but the fellow he had been partners with in the sawmilling business had taken off with most of the season's profits. He'd heard this partner was in Edmonton, and when George's friend told us who this fellow was, the light clicked on for me.

Shortly before we embarked on this trip to the Yukon, I was out with some of the Camsell Hospital crew and this guy, who was with Rita Murphy, was really playing the big timer. He was buying drinks for the whole party and had a roll of big bills in his pocket that would choke a hippopotamus. When George's friend told us how he had been ripped off, I immediately conjured up a picture of this great big roll of bills his ex-partner was flashing in Edmonton. I thought, "How ironic," so we bought our friend another drink.

Next morning we headed down the Alaska Highway and had an uneventful, somewhat monotonous trip back to Edmonton and the Camsell Hospital. I gathered what belongings I had, and with some of my summer's pay bought a Canadian Pacific Airlines ticket to Victoria, where the Jubilee Hospital would be my home for the next year while I went through my junior internship and discovered obstetrics and gynaecology (ob-gyn). Dr. Falconer and the other doctors on staff wanted the department to give me an airline ticket back to Vancouver as a bonus, but the business manager, an Ottawa bureaucrat, said no, it might set a precedent, so they could not do it. The s.o.b.

## Wolf in Maternity Clothing

In a typical shift in the Ob-Gyn service, a car would pull up to the front door, a woman would stagger through the door to the waiting stretcher, and she would be transported up to the obstetrics floor where Miss O'Brien, the head nurse, called orders to her staff like a sergeant major. If the delivery was imminent, the patient would go right to the delivery room, someone would call the obstetrician, someone would be getting the patient undressed, and, if her pains were severe, someone would grab a Trilene anaesthetic mask and hold that on her face to slow down the contractions. The patient always seemed to have her suitcase at the top of the stretcher beside her head.

One day Don Horton, another intern, and I decided to stage an unrehearsed trial run for the maternity department. I got on the stretcher with a couple of pillows on my belly to produce the desired contour and covered myself with a sheet. I had a very grotesque wolf mask on my face, but placed the usual suitcase at the head of the stretcher so that you couldn't see my face until you were right beside me. Horton phoned from the first floor to tell them that he was bringing up a maternity case all ready to deliver.

On our way up on the elevator I howled like a wounded cougar so that they could hear me all the way to the top floor. The elevator door opened and Horton steered me towards the case room, with me yowling in a high-pitched voice.

O'Brien immediately went into action. She called extra nurses to help, was snapping orders to do this and do that, and bounded into the delivery room to tell the patient (me) to stop pushing; she snatched the suitcase off the stretcher and was just bending over to give some soothing words when she came face to face with a wolf-man.

Her reaction was instantaneous—and lethal. "Goddamn you, Holley!" she howled and grabbed the Trilene mask, clapping it over my face with a valve wide open. I got a couple of good drags of the stuff before I managed to squirm off the stretcher; about one more whiff and I would have been on my way to dreamland. What a terrifying thought: to be anaesthetized and at the mercy of that bunch of women!

Unfortunately, the rest of my junior internship wasn't very interesting. There were seven of us interns and we rotated through all the various

*The Royal Jubilee interns take a break: (from left to right) Cort MacKenzie, R. Stojan, R. Sargent, Brody Coulles, Don Horton, Al Holley, Ron Bonnell.*

services, for which we were on 24-hour call every other night. Compared to other hospital jobs I have had we didn't work too hard, but we didn't get taught too much either. The best training that I had was on the Ob-Gyn service, where the staff actually put themselves out to teach us, especially on the obstetrics side.

Miss Plunkett was the supervisor of the obstetrics department. The head nurse, who was present at most of the deliveries during the daylight hours, was tall, attractive, and vivacious Irene O'Brien.

At one time during the year I staged a one-man protest on the surgery service to get to do a little surgery on my own, under supervision. I guess it must have had some effect, as one of the surgeons let me do an appendectomy. Something like that was all I wanted. As I mentioned earlier, the Royal Jubilee was not a great teaching hospital at that time, although it had a very good nurses training school.

Victoria was a pleasant place to live, but it was not my kind of country. There were no real challenges, no dangerous animals except for maybe some members of the nursing school.

# EIGHT

# Ni_díge'jon, "Like-Medicine-Man"

When I left Indian Health Services after my last summer job I had told Dr. Falconer that when I finished my internship and had my licence to practise, I would run an outpost hospital for them for a year since they had given me some good summer jobs. I knew they always had trouble getting doctors to go into these isolated places. I told them that I would go anywhere they needed someone, but I would like the worst place they had.

They needed someone at the outpost hospital at Fort Rae, NWT, on Marion Lake, just north of Great Slave Lake. The settlement was 100 miles from Yellowknife by canoe in summer or 75 miles over the trail by dog team in winter. It was also accessible by floatplane in summer or by a plane with skis in winter. For a month in the early winter during freeze-up and for about six weeks during break-up in the spring, aircraft were unable to land, so residents were pretty well left to their own devices during those times.

Fort Rae consisted of the Catholic mission church with three priests and a brother who ran their diesel power plant and was a general handyman. There was a two-man RCMP detachment, a wildlife warden, a government schoolteacher and his wife, a Hudson's Bay Company post with a manager and his wife, and a young HBC clerk fresh out from Edinburgh. An order of Roman Catholic nuns from Quebec operated the hospital, which had about 70 patients. I would be the only doctor. Fine, I said, I would take it.

About 1,800 Dogrib lived in the area, but they were pretty nomadic. People were scattered all the way from Yellowknife to Fort Reliance at the east end of Great Slave; to Rae and to Fort Providence at the head of the Mackenzie River at the west end of the lake; and running northwest to

Lac La Martre and northeast to the edge of the barren lands. They usually all came in to Fort Rae at Christmas and Easter.

I hunted ducks in the fall on occasion with some of the younger guys and got to be on pretty good terms with most of them, as well as most of the white people. The nursing sisters were good to work with. I had a handyman who cut my wood and cleaned my house; he was also my interpreter. He spoke Dogrib, Chipewyan, Slavey, French, and English and was a good man.

## Mercy Trip

In November 1952 we were running short of streptomycin at the hospital. It had arrived in Yellowknife but was sitting there waiting for the planes to start flying. We had no guarantee of when that would be. Moreover, none of us had our Christmas liquor. We decided to make a trip to Yellowknife by dog team. Dog rental was a dollar a day per dog, so a six-dog team cost us $6 a day. Frozen or dried jackfish cost us a dollar a stick, which was six fish strung on a willow stick. The dogs got one fish every night.

Five teams made up the convoy: Bob Douglas, wildlife warden; Jess Lafferty, his Native patrolman; Constable Benger, RCMP; a humpback guy called "Humpy"; and myself. By this time I had a Native name, "Ni_dige'jon," which meant "Like-Medicine-Man." I rented a team from Henry Lafferty, and Al Benger also rented a team: the others had their own dogs. We travelled on the overland trail, which took us to Maurice Blackduck's camp, 50 miles from Rae and 25 miles to Yellowknife.

We all bunked in at Maurice's cabin, the five of us with him and his family. We flopped our sleeping bags on the floor and were so glad to be in a nice warm cabin that the hard floor didn't bother us at all. Everyone in the camp was glad to trade us rabbit stew for our canned food. We were happy with that and left them some extra tea and sugar as a bonus. Anyone who is travelling in the Arctic or sub-Arctic in the winter could make their own camp all right, but a warm cabin or igloo always looks pretty good when you come in tired off the trail.

The trip so far was uneventful, and we made good time, doing the 50 miles that first day. We were travelling along the edge of a river and I broke through the ice with one foot, getting cold and wet to my knee. When I went through I quickly pulled the foot and leg out and threw myself on the back of the toboggan. I yelled at the dogs to "Hottah," which the Dogribs used in place of "mush." The trail veered towards shore just there and we were soon on solid ground. The two Native men really impressed me with how quickly they got up to me, got my wet sock and mukluk off, and got a dry sock and liner out of my pack and on my foot.

*Fort Rae! The buildings were clustered on a reef of smooth, round-topped bedrock that extended out into shallow Marian Lake. In winter, Ft. Rae was cold and windswept; in summer, it was free of mosquitoes and flies.*

The swiftness of their action left me speechless. They had my greatest admiration after that.

We made it on into Yellowknife in good time, part of the trail being on the hard-packed snow of Great Slave Lake. We were glad the weather was clear with no wind when we were travelling on the open lake. Being on the open ice of Great Slave in the winter is much like being on the Arctic Ocean ice. You try not to waste much time.

In Yellowknife I arranged to pick up my streptomycin from the Indian agent, and we got the Christmas liquor for the whole white settlement. Native bands were still interdicted up there. We left our dogs at the village, where the two Native men looked after feeding them along with their own, while we stayed in town.

Benger and I booked in at the Yellowknife Hotel; a good hot soak in the bathtub felt great. We were invited to a party at the nurses' residence on Saturday night. We had a great time, and even though we drank our fair share, our behaviour was nothing less than exemplary. We hoped that if we behaved well we might get invited again. We had a drink at the Yellowknife Hotel bar, and met the head barmaid, a good sort who had grubstaked more than one guy who was down on his luck.

After a few days of R&R we packed the toboggans and headed back on the trail. I rolled the streptomycin up in my sleeping bag to keep it from freezing. We made Maurice Blackduck's camp the first afternoon, leaving early next morning for Fort Rae while the weather was still good.

*We met with Maurice and Marie Sanschagrin during our trip to Yellowknife. She was a medicine woman who unfortunately died in hospital soon afterwards.*

We trotted right along—I kept out of the water this time. We stopped at suppertime, chewed some dried meat, and made a pot of tea. By the time we got on the trail again it was dark, turning out to be a clear and frosty night except for the Milky Way and a sliver of moon. The Northern Lights were putting on a great show.

These old trail men had a custom: when travelling at night or when visibility was bad, the lead team would stop every three or four miles and wait for everybody to catch up to make sure they were all present and accounted for. If someone was missing, a couple of the faster teams would hike back and check on them. Sometimes one might get a lame dog or do something dumb and go through the ice like I did. We never had to go down the back trail for anybody, but stopped regularly for everyone to catch up.

About the second stop, someone pulled out a bottle of V.O. and passed it around. We all had a snort, including the Native guys. Even though Al was a member of the RCMP and I was a justice of the peace, we knew that this was not a time to be picky about the Dogribs being interdicted, especially when they were as good as we were, or better, at what we were doing. When you are out on the trail you pull together and are all equal unless and until you prove otherwise. So we just kept up our steady dogtrot, running behind for awhile to get warm and also to make it easier on the dogs, then jumping on to ride until we got our wind. And every few miles we stopped to let the stragglers catch up, each time having a nip out of someone's jug. We were within sight of the lights of the settlement when we tucked the last empty bottle into the toboggan.

*This is part of the five-team convoy that mushed to Yellowknife in November 1952.*

I made a special note to myself that even though we each had consumed 26 ounces, we were all perfectly sober—shows how much whisky a man can burn up while chasing after a dog team on a frosty night.

It was a good trip, with everyone glad to see us when we got back.

I found that in the north, when the weather is bad, everybody settles down in cabins and tents and nobody goes very far except to cut firewood and get some snow to melt for water. They never embarked on any long trips until the weather moderated, though the bush pilots sometimes flew when it was pretty cold.

One day I flew with Dave Floyd in a Norseman from Fort Rae to Yellowknife when it was –58 degrees F. Dave had come out with some supplies for the settlement, and it so happened that I had admitted a two-week-old baby that morning, sick with pneumonia. I thought this little kid would have a better chance if we got her out to the Yellowknife hospital where they were better equipped to look after her than we were. So we bundled her up and took her with us. We got her in a taxi and up to the hospital. When we arrived at the hospital, the doctor on duty didn't want to admit her because he thought she might bring measles to the hospital. But I knew he didn't want to admit her because she was "just an Indian kid." I told him that he would admit her or I would cold-cock him in his tracks. She survived and was back in the settlement after she recovered.

## "Oui, Docteur"

Another group of patients we had to exercise our expertise on at regular intervals were kids with tuberculosis meningitis, usually young boys about six to ten years old. They all used to die prior to the advent of streptomycin. The recommended treatment, which we followed, was to give this antibiotic into the spinal fluid daily the first week, then every second day, decreasing to once a week to once a month thereafter. These were usually kids that were in hospital with active pulmonary TB.

The sisters were really sharp at picking up these cases, and it was to their good nursing care that we could attribute our relatively good results compared to the city hospitals. The sister-in-charge would tell me that she was worried about young Alexis or Jimmie—he was moping around the last few days and didn't want to eat, was nauseated, and just not right. The sisters were quite diplomatic. They would not say, "I think this kid has meningitis, are you going to do something about it?" Instead they would hover around and give me a questioning look, and when I said, "Do you think he might have meningitis?" they would say, "Oui, Docteur," with the most relieved look on their face that I had agreed with their diagnosis. And they were usually right.

I used to feel sorry for those little kids when they saw me coming into the ward. They knew that it was going to be painful, even though I slipped some local in first. Having had repeated spinal taps when I was a kid, I knew what it was like. I must say you get pretty slick at a procedure when you do it every day, and I tried to be as slick and as fast as I could.

I think our survival rate was almost 100 percent, which quite impressed the folks at the Camsell Hospital in Edmonton. I don't know what the long-term results were. I think the sisters prayed pretty hard for these kids, and that was always fine with me; I was glad to have any help we could get.

In our hospital, with the high rate of TB in the population, everything was tuberculosis until proven otherwise. If a man came in with a swollen, red knee, your first diagnosis was tuberculosis synovitis rather than a sprained knee. If a young fellow came in with a swollen testicle, you would first think of tuberculous epididymitis.

There had been a doctor in Fort Rae for a year before I got there; he was the first and I was the second doctor in the area. By the time I left, the death rate had dropped by 300 percent. This was due to several factors: first, we had been able to get streptomycin, INH, and PAS, all anti-tuberculosis drugs, which hitherto had not been available. Second, we had made our presence known and indicated that we were there to help the people. Third, I don't know about the other doctor, but I used to go out to some of their camps, usually travelling with the RCMP by dog team. I hunted and fished with the locals, gaining their friendship and confidence. We got the women coming in to the hospital to have their babies, and that was a step in reducing infant mortality. (The Native women never seemed to have their babies in the middle of the night; they almost always had them in the daylight. I delivered one white woman in the hospital and she, of course, had her baby at four in the morning.)

One of the best compliments I ever had was when the regional supervisor came up from Edmonton on a tour of inspection. The Native women made a delegation to ask him to keep me there at Fort Rae. I was quite touched.

There was very little trauma at the hospital. One young man slipped and broke his ankle while chasing a girl around her cabin on New Year's Day, and a trapper broke his finger setting a muskrat trap. If there was more trauma, I didn't hear about it.

Medicine men and women were active. One old woman was the main Medicine Person (politically correct), but she was admitted to hospital with pulmonary haemorrhage and advanced TB, and I think that after I left she died in the hospital.

We used to get the odd case of gonorrhoea, mostly when the weather was good and someone travelled to Yellowknife or elsewhere "outside." Otherwise our population was pretty isolated from outside influences.

One time a somewhat fast-moving Native doll from Yellowknife came to the settlement. In short order I found out how people entertained themselves during the long winter nights. After a couple of days, when it appeared that the gonorrhoea outbreak was assuming epidemic proportions, I called in my handyman interpreter, Joe, and we drew up a plan of action. I made a big chart and on it we entered the names of all the young men who had come in for treatment for gonorrhoea. Then Joe was dispatched into the settlement to round them all up so that we could get the names of their contacts. With that information on the chart, Joe went back out to bring in all these female contacts. These women were all given a good shot of penicillin and told to lay off the love life for ten days, and from them we got the names of all their contacts and Joe brought them all in.

Within two or three days we had a chart that spread out like the branches of a family tree. Then the tree started narrowing down. There were no new cases, only a few reinfections. When the last case appeared to be cleared up, we declared the epidemic was over. We were glad that it was winter and that riverboat traffic was not running on the Mackenzie or we would have been chasing dosed-up people all the way from Fort Chipewyan to Inuvik.

There were the occasional language problems due to lack of improper interpretation. One evening an old lady arrived at my door accompanied by some friends. They were all quite upset about something, jabbering away in a Dogrib dialect that I didn't understand. A group of teenage girls were close by so I got one of them to come over. I knew that she could speak English because she went to the day school. I asked her to find out what was the old lady's problem. After a lengthy discussion the girl told me that the woman had some kind of diarrhoea. I said, "Fine, we can fix that up; come with me to the hospital dispensary." In the dispensary I mixed a bottle of chokem-up and handed it to her. She took it very reluctantly; in fact, I had to press the bottle in her hand and usher her out the door.

I watched them go out the door and head down the trail, obviously not satisfied. The first person they met was old Michel Bouvier, the RCMP interpreter. I went out and asked Michel what the old lady's problem was. After some further discussion, Michel, with a little smile on his face, told me that she had lost her old-age pension cheque. I could just hear her and her friends saying, "That crazy doctor!"

## Courtroom Dramas

Supplying justice was not one of my priorities in the north, but as justice of the peace I had some obligation to be involved at times. The RCMP boys who were stationed in these areas had a lot more common sense than you will find in the judiciary system "outside." Up here it did not matter if you had money for a high-priced lawyer because there usually were no lawyers in the area. There certainly weren't any in Fort Rae or any of the other outposts.

I heard stories about travesties of justice imposed on the Native people by federally appointed judges trying to apply "white man's justice" to people of a different culture, often with political involvement in the findings and outcome. I admired the RCMP boys; they avoided imposing their ideas of justice or attitudes in court cases.

Usually the results of the cases were foregone conclusions, known equally by the accused persons and the Mounties whose duty it was to apprehend them and be involved in their prosecutions. As justice of the peace I saw that they got a fair trial without vindictiveness on the part of the Mounties or of the mission priests, who were responsible for reporting many of the misdemeanours that brought the culprits to trial.

I was limited, of course, in what types of charges I could handle. Serious offences like murder, rape, or civil charges had to be sent to a stipendiary magistrate at Fort Smith, which, being the capital of the Territories, was home to higher-class bureaucrats than me.

On one occasion the old priest went stomping over to the RCMP office demanding that we charge a young Native man. The priest reported that this fellow had pursued a Native girl around her cabin with an amorous glint in his eye, and in the heat of the chase had bowled over the old grandfather.

The two Mounties came over for a conference: not about proposed punishments, but about technicalities. They had found that if we charged the defendant as demanded by the priest, I could not oversee the case. Instead he would have to go to Fort Smith to be tried by the stipendiary magistrate. We suspected he would be convicted of attempted rape on the girl and assault causing bodily harm on the old grandpa. The young defendant would be flown there on a charter flight with one of our

*Michel Bouvier was the RCMP interpreter. He helped me diagnose an old woman's problem—a missing pension cheque—after my initial diagnosis of diarrhoea.*

Mounties to accompany him, all at taxpayers' expense. He would likely be found guilty and would be in jail for the rest of the winter, enjoying a warm bed and good food, better than he would have at home. And he would be splitting firewood and cutting ice on the river, all for the detachment over there.

We unanimously agreed that we would change the charge a little to better suit the interests of justice and the economy of the community. Court was duly called, the Mounties were in their scarlet tunics with boots polished, and the J.P. (me) even wore a suit and tie. Old Michel was sworn in as interpreter. Bob Douglas, wildlife warden, attended as a friend of the court and testified to the good character and lack of previous offences of the accused. One Mountie acted as prosecutor, the other as court clerk and bailiff. They called various witnesses and we had difficulty keeping the noise down to a dull roar.

The defendant pleaded guilty to the reduced charge of creating a disturbance and was duly fined $25. That was a considerable amount in 1952; we considered it to be a suitable deterrent. In this day and age the feminists in this country would have me dangling by the testicles for rendering such a verdict, but there were none of them trapping around Fort Rae at the time, fortunately.

Snow's Criminal Code of Canada was supposed to guide me. It set definite limits to when a magistrate or J.P. must order a fine or imprisonment for the various offences, along with minimum and maximum sentences—there was not much leeway for a judge to get carried away with imaginative penalties.

A case that we had over at Fort Providence gave me some misgivings because I thought the prescribed minimum penalty was too severe. The local priest turned in a citizen to the RCMP, a free trader (i.e., independent of the HBC), who the priest alleged gave an Indian some liquor; apparently the Indian became drunk and disorderly. The trader pleaded guilty so the case was brief. When I looked up the charge in Snow's Criminal Code I found the minimum penalty was a fine of $200. In 1952 I knew that $200 represented half the trader's income for the year. However, I had no recourse but to lay it on him. I told him it was the minimum and he took it with good grace.

On my next monthly trip to Providence I saw this trader on the docket again. When the boys sent in the $200 and the summary of the case, their superior officer at headquarters noted that in evidence it was stated that the liquor supplied was homebrew. This hotshot sent the boys at Providence a very snotty memo stating that they had been remiss in their duties and that the man must also be charged under Article 4235 of the Northwest Territories Liquor Act for making moonshine, contrary to the Act. So here we were again. They had kept a bottle of the moonshine as a court specimen and this was produced. I heard that according to the Territories Liquor Act, if two witnesses each smelled the contents of a bottle and declared it was alcoholic, it was alcoholic and the courts accepted this. In this case, the contents were declared to be moonshine and therefore alcohol and the accused was found guilty. He had no comment. That night there was a party at the RCMP barracks, and the trader was there with the rest of us. We did not talk shop.

I was supposed to get so much for every case that I sat on, to be paid by the federal government, but I never did receive any money.

## NINE

# Hottah!

When the worst of the weather was over, Constable Al Benger and I decided we should do a dog-team patrol out on the barren lands to Snare River, where there was a hydro dam. This hydroelectric plant supplied power to the mines and the town of Yellowknife, and the crew did not have much contact with anyone.

We were able to get a good dog team from a Dogrib man who earlier in the winter had taken some Army personnel from Great Slave Lake to Great Bear Lake and back. There were seven dogs in the team, all big strong brutes and in good condition from their trip to Great Bear and back. The dogs were not pets by any means, but they knew how to pull a load.

We figured it would take us three days for 60 miles each way, so we bought dried fish from the locals to last us seven or eight days. We calculated food for ourselves for a week; we could get some extra rations at the power site if we needed them. We packed our Arctic Three-Star sleeping bags, our rifles, a change of dry clothes, and a compass each as well as matches and maps. We wrapped the whole load in a big tarp and tied it into the twelve-foot toboggan.

After leaving instructions with the other Mountie and the wildlife warden on how we planned to go and when we expected to start back, we left by a dog trail through the muskeg at the back of the settlement. We came out onto the open ice at Russell Lake, three or four miles beyond the settlement.

I chased the dogs for the first shift, standing on the small platform of the toboggan, which stuck out behind the load. My rifle was tacked just under the tarp and my snowshoes were tied on the top of the load. Constable Benger trotted along on his light trail snowshoes some distance behind.

*Constable Al Benger and I are on our way to Snare River.*

When we were two or three miles out on the open lake, a big red malamute in the team looked around at me and growled—a low throaty growl. He was second from the lead. This went on for a while; he would look at me over his shoulder and growl a little more. I really wanted to keep them moving, but I thought if I tripped and fell or had to stop for any reason, he would drag the whole team back on me. I didn't need that, and Benger was too far behind to do me any good, so I yelled, "Whoa," and sank the snow hook into the packed snow.

With my heavy caribou-hide mitts on I went up to the red dog, undid the bellyband, and pulled the harness off him. I grabbed him by the collar and dragged him out of the team, back to the head of the toboggan. There I pulled the wheel dog out of harness and put old Red in his place. This way the grumpy red son-of-a-bitch was anchored to the front of the toboggan and he wouldn't go far. I put the black-and-white wheel dog up front in the vacant spot. Working in the wheel dog position was the hardest job on the team. I pulled up the snow hook that served as an anchor and was ready to go again when Benger caught up. I yelled, "Hottah!" and the team lunged forward.

Next thing, I ran up and cracked that red dog a couple of good ones right across the ass with my shot-loaded whip. Every time he slacked up I got him a couple more. That was the end of his growls and dirty looks. I told Benger about the incident, so when he got on the back of the toboggan in my place he carried on and gave that dog a few more.

We travelled all day, up Russell Lake and then over Slemon Lake, a big lake about 25 miles long. At the east end of Slemon Lake we followed

*The dogs rest as Const. Benger and I snowshoe ahead to break a trail for the dog-team.*

a portage trail through an area of poplar and willow growth where the wind had blown in loose snow over a foot deep. We had to get out our snowshoes to break trail for the dogs.

The lead man used a big pair of snowshoes, with the other man using the smaller trail snowshoes, leading the team behind. We eventually got to a sheltered area with some dry wood, birch trees and bark, for building a fire. Benger, our dogs, and I were so tired we stopped for the night. We chained the dogs close in around our little camp because there were lots of wolves around. We weren't worried about them bothering us, but we knew they would sure get our dogs if we didn't keep them close. We fed the dogs half a frozen fish each, made a fire on which we heated up a can of beef stew, and boiled a pot of coffee. Then we dug out a hole in the snow with our snowshoes, big enough for our two sleeping bags, and we lined it with some spruce boughs in the bottom, then the tarp, and then spread our bedrolls.

By the time we ate and drank our coffee, it was dark and time to turn in. We laid our rifles one on each side of our sleeping bags, took off our outer clothing, which we laid between the bags and the tarp, crawled in with our long-johns and our inner socks on, and snuggled in for the night. There was some extra length to the big tarp, so we pulled this up from the bottom over our bags to keep out any snow. We were quite comfortable and soon asleep. I awoke during the night a few times with the stars shining above us and the wolves howling on the lakes on both sides of us. I turned over and went back to sleep.

Morning came and the weather was good. We crawled out of our sleeping bags, made a fire, toasted the homemade bread we got from the wildlife warden's girlfriend, barbecued a frozen whitefish over the fire, and made some more coffee.

We packed our bedrolls and gear, wrapped the tarp around it, and got ready to go. Before stuffing our rifles under the tarp we glassed all around to see if we could see a wolf to shoot. There were none in sight. We put a feed of fish in a gunny sack for the dogs on our return trip, climbed up a poplar tree, and hung it about twelve feet off the ground.

We took a good look at our map and individually checked our compass bearings, which both turned out the same, for which we were happy.

In the next stage of our journey we had to cross one lake east of our camp, then follow the next lake in a northeasterly direction to its end. Then we would cross a short portage through the jack pines, which should take us out to the old power line running from Snare River dam to Yellowknife. An old construction caboose, hauled in by cat in the wintertime, was marked on the map.

We chased the dogs through the scrub timber to the first lake to the east of us, crossed that one, and went across another portage to the longer lake on the map, running to the northeast. Hard-blown snow on this second lake made good going for the dogs. The drag line behind the toboggan was in easy reach so that if the dogs took off across the lake after a wolf or a fox we would not get left behind.

All the dogsleds and toboggans used by northern mushers had a brake you could jump on; it dug into the frozen snow and soon brought the dogs to a halt. Most of the dogs knew the word "Whoa" and would stop unless there was something very interesting ahead of them. If the brake wouldn't stop them, you dumped the toboggan on its side and ran up to jump on the side of the head of the toboggan. With that digging in they usually didn't run far.

We did see one wolf during the morning—on the shore of the lake about 600 yards away. We stopped and I took a shot at it with my .270 Winchester but missed. Benger didn't bother to try with his RCMP issue 30:30 carbine, which of course was not much good over 300 yards.

We travelled for over half a day on the lakes and then turned right where the trail pointed east-northeast through the jack pines. After a mile through the scrub jack pines and spruce we came onto the power line, which ran pretty well north and south. We followed this for a couple hours of heavy going and came to the old caboose. We knew we were only two or three hours from the Snare River dam and camp.

We tied the dogs and had a look at the caboose: there was a woodstove in the cabin with some dry wood, four wooden bunks, two windows with glass in them, and a roof with no holes. A phone line connected the power dam to the gold mines at Yellowknife; there were crank telephones nailed on the wall in each of the cabins along the line.

We both knew at a glance that the caboose would be our Snare River Hilton for the night. We pulled the toboggan up to the cabin, then tied our dogs up close by. We unloaded our stuff and threw it inside where it would be safe. You have to be careful when you are travelling with dogs. If one or two get loose they will clean out anything edible on your sleigh or toboggan, including buckskin or rawhide, in pretty short order. You can take your food into the tent if you don't have anywhere else to put it. But if you are travelling in bear country any time other than midwinter, you do *not* put food anywhere near your tent unless you want to have a bear as a guest for midnight supper. We gave the dogs half a frozen fish each (about three pounds) and then got a good fire going in the old stove.

The cabin, by the way, was not locked. This is the rule with these cabins along trails in isolated places, as it may mean the difference between survival or not for anyone needing to use them. There was no food in the place, which was okay with us; we had food. But there was a coal oil lamp, which we found handy, and some candles. We cooked supper, melted snow for coffee and to wash the dishes, and bedded down.

Before we went to bed, Benger tried out the telephone and was able to raise the guys at the power dam camp. He told them who and where we were and that we would be in by noon next day. Hearing someone's voice on a phone away out in this God-forsaken caboose only seemed to heighten our isolation and the loneliness of our little spot on a large map far from just about everywhere. Snare River, on the edge of the barren lands, was certainly out of the high-rent district, but we were even quite a distance from there. Regardless of all these depressing factors, we slept soundly, only keeping an ear open for the sound of dogs being attacked by wolves.

In the morning we ate breakfast, cleaned up a little, since this was an opportunity to have hot water, then we cleaned up the cabin and loaded the toboggan for the last leg of the journey to Snare River. We hitched the dogs and headed them up the winter cat trail along the power line to Snare River. We saw one wolf out in the open and I took a shot at it, but it was too far away to expect to hit it on the move with open sights. When we got in sight of camp we urged the dogs on with loud "Hottahs" and a crack of the whip and entered the yard at a brisk trot.

When you are dog-teaming it in the north and are visiting someone's camp, it is customary to arrive and depart with a great flurry of action, even if your dogs have been dragging their asses for the last three miles. The dogs seem to accept and enjoy this routine and muster enough energy to put on the show.

At the power station we were greeted warmly as we were the only visitors they had all winter, with the exception of bush pilot Ernie Boffa, who had dropped off the mail from Yellowknife a couple of times. We stayed for two days, enough to rest ourselves and our dogs; had some good food (even pie put out by the camp cook); then said goodbye to everyone before heading our dogs down the back trail to Fort Rae.

The weather stayed good and we stayed over at the line cabin the first night, left early next morning, and arrived in good time at our previous camp, where we had left dog food in the tree. It was a good thing that we tied it high in the tree, as the snow was packed down all around the bottom of the tree where the wolves evidently smelled it and were doing their darndest to get it down. We fed the dogs from the cached fish and hung the rest back up until morning. Benger and I chained our dogs up closer than usual, since we expected the wolves might come in pretty close because they knew there was food in camp. We put our tarp and sleeping bags in the same hole in the snow that we used on the way up, and slept soundly.

In the morning, after breakfast and breaking camp, we headed out through the portage where we had broken trail coming in. This heavy section was easier this time. We came out on Slemon Lake and followed our tracks to its bottom end and southwest corner. The only trouble we had was a touch of snow blindness out on the lake, where there was nothing except blazing white

*Trail dogs could get pretty grumpy. Bob Douglas insisted that his wolf "Shorty," was tame (shown here). I was glad this trail dog was on a chain.*

reflection off the endless snow. We were glad to have sunglasses. At the end of Slemon Lake we took the portage trail over to the smaller Russell Lake, and shortly before sundown we trotted our dogs off the trail and tied up at the RCMP barracks. I hiked over to the hospital as soon as I had a hot bath and got into some clean clothes.

We were gone for a week and came back with the dogs and ourselves in good shape. Al Benger and I developed a closer friendship after the trip. A weeklong winter dog-team trek brings out some of the best and the worst in a man. It is not an exercise for wimps, nor is this a country where they would thrive. We both pulled our weight, as did the dogs. Even the grumpy red dog got friendlier as time went on. Benger was more trail wise at winter travelling than I was, and many of the things he suggested kept us out of trouble, I'm sure.

## Squeaky and the Otoscope

On a miserable stormy Saturday afternoon the HBC trader sent a Native boy over to tell me that the Indian agent in Yellowknife had sent a radio message: a woman in a camp at Lac la Martre was haemorrhaging. Would I fly out with a bush pilot and see what it was? I sent a message back that I would be ready to go when the plane arrived. I grabbed my Arctic sleeping bag, in which I stuffed some extra warm clothing, and humped my stuff over to the RCMP barracks—close to where the aircraft usually landed.

Lac la Martre was about 40 miles northwest of Fort Rae, between Great Slave and Great Bear lakes. It was a big lake, 20 miles long. We took off and soon were circling the desolate, windswept winter camp on a narrow point of land jutting out into the lake.

We were flying an old Beaver aircraft on skis, and when we landed we taxied up to the camp, which was a group of tents, each banked up on all sides with three or four feet of snow and willow brush to break the wind. Thin wisps of smoke were coming from stovepipe chimneys. Sled dogs curled up nose to bunghole in snowdrifts around the camp.

We went into the tent where the sick woman was lying on some blankets on a pile of spruce boughs. The tent was warm from a fire in an airtight heater. A group of Dogrib women sat around on spruce boughs on the floor. One woman who spoke English told me that the woman had passed some stuff with big clots and her bleeding had since pretty well stopped.

She was pale, but not bad; her pulse and blood pressure were normal. I examined her belly and found her uterus to be just a little enlarged but firm. She was not bleeding. It looked like she had aborted and was bleeding until she passed the placenta, but the emergency was now over.

I gave her a shot of longlasting penicillin to control any infection and a shot of Ergometrin to help keep her uterus clamped down. I left her some Ergotrate tablets to take for five days and told her to rest for three to four days. She and the others seemed to appreciate our coming out. I told her that if she was having any more trouble, such as more bleeding, they could wrap her up and put her on a toboggan and have her at the hospital in Fort Rae in a day and a half. They had lots of sled dogs. I knew her heavy bleeding should be over, and any more bleeding would be from retained fragments of placenta; in that case we would have to get her into hospital to do a D&C (scrape out the fragments) in order to stop her bleeding completely. She would stand the trip in, I was sure. The service compared favourably with the waiting time for surgery that we currently enjoy in our politician-organized healthcare system.

By the time Squeaky, the pilot, and I got to our plane, it had suddenly become dusk, and the weather had improved some, with the wind dying down. Squeak, which was the nickname we had given him because of his high-pitched voice, asked, "What do you think, Doc? Shall we stay till daylight in the morning or go?"

It didn't take me long to decide how I would vote. We could either stay in this windswept flea-and-louse-ridden camp or we could get to Yellowknife, where I knew there was a party on. I said, "Let's get the hell out of here." We hiked to the plane and found the skis frozen down. That happens. The two of us took hold of the tail of the Beaver and wiggled it back and forth until the skis broke loose. Then I kept the skis moving from side to side until Squeak got the motor revved up and taxied slowly out onto the lake. I ran beside the plane until I was sure we wouldn't have to stop, then I jumped on a ski and climbed up into the cabin while the plane was moving. I slammed the door shut and we took off. It was just light enough to see the tree line on the opposite shore. We gained altitude and turned back the way we had come, toward Rae and then the Yellowknife airport.

But we had a problem. We didn't have any lights on the plane, neither landing lights nor cabin lights. My faithful pilot asked, "Have you got any kind of a gadget with a light so I can read my instrument panel?" I dug out my otoscope from my bag, figuring that if it was good enough to see in ears, I could take the fine tip off and we should be able to read the instruments. It worked well and he found everything to be working; we checked the compass bearing, and after five minutes of flying we could see the beacon on the tower at Yellowknife. A scrap of a half moon came out through the clouds and we knew that we were on our way. I gave a quiet thanks to Welch-Allyn instrument company and the good long-life batteries they put in their otoscopes.

We flew straight toward the airport beacon until we got almost to Yellowknife, then veered off towards Yellowknife Bay, where we had five miles of ice to land on. As we flew over the edge of town towards the bay, the moon disappeared behind the clouds and we were really in the dark. We knew where the bay was and that we were heading right to it, but we could not see the ice that we hoped to land on. We just hoped there was nothing parked out there.

I shone the light on the instrument panel and Squeak eased her down and down, throttling her back in the darkness, until he felt the skis touch the snow. He gave the throttle a push to pick up the ski tips and let her settle onto the snow while we came to a gradual stop. Squeaky spun her around and with his head out the side window we taxied the old Beaver slowly up to the Associated Airways shop and shut her down.

I caught a ride to the hotel, where I cleaned up and ate supper. I had somehow lost interest in any party, so I had a nightcap at the bar and went up to bed. There wasn't much else going on next morning, so I got one of the boys to fly me back to Fort Rae.

## Northern Haute Cuisine

There wasn't much to do in the fort, so I invited the other bachelors over for dinner one Sunday night. Spring approached, and the Natives were busy trapping or shooting muskrat and beaver. I got my man, Joe, to get me a half dozen muskrats that he skinned and dressed out for me. Dinner featured several kinds of before-dinner and after-dinner drinks, and the entree was not southern fried chicken but northern fried muskrat.

Muskrat, cut in pieces and dredged in flour with seasoning, tasted much like wild duck. The pieces were placed in a large frying pan in which a generous amount of bacon grease was melted along with finely sliced garlic, seasoned with poultry seasoning with added sage, thyme, and tarragon. It was served on a pilaf of brown rice with assorted vegetables from as many cans as we could make available, and everyone said it was delicious.

We didn't have any wine for this feast, and mixer was scarce in that country due to the freight. We featured a special drink of the house made of rye and creme de menthe. We called it a Green Dragon because after three drinks you looked green and your ass was dragg'n.

All of the Natives ate lots of muskrat and beaver this time of year when the ice was melting and there were leads of open water to hunt on. When you were travelling in a canoe close to shore, the Native kids would be sitting sunning themselves after a long winter. Having subsisted on a low-fat diet of mostly caribou and rabbits all winter, they really thrived on some meat with fat in it, like beaver. These kids looked happy and healthy and their skin even looked oily when you saw them in spring camps after the ice had started to open up and they got some fat in their diet.

## "Do You Mind If I Smoke, Doc?"

Spring came—time to make another trip to Fort Providence. The Indian agent arranged for a charter that duly arrived at Rae to pick me up. I was not likely to have any patients to transport, and there were no court

*Caribou run over Yellowknife Bay. The Dogrib hunted caribou far inland to the barrens in the northeast. Photo by Henry Busse, who later went missing in the Barren Lands.*

cases waiting for me, so on this flight they sent a little Cessna 172. I didn't like flying in these small planes and much preferred the larger and more powerful DeHavilland Beaver. Later that day we were happy enough to have its smaller wingspread.

When we got to Providence the small military airstrip was mostly cleared of snow by the warm spring winds, and the gravel was showing though. My friend Squeaky was flying me again. We decided we would fly over to the Mackenzie River, close to where it drained out of the lake, and land on a snye (backwater) just below the residential school. To our dismay we found that when the river came up it had broken up the ice in the snye, and large chunks four feet thick were scattered around like the Maginot line. So the snye was not an option.

We didn't have enough gas to get all the way back to Fort Rae, so we thought we would take a tour out over the lake to see how far we would have to walk back to the post. We were flying low over the end of the strip when two soldiers came out of a hut and were waving us towards the muskeg and scrub spruce behind the settlement. We didn't quite understand their signals, but Squeak banked the plane sharply and we flew over to where they were pointing. Then we saw what they meant. A winter cat trail cleared a narrow swath through the spruce, with snow in the cat tracks.

We made a wide circle to come in on a straight stretch of the trail, aiming our skis for the cat tracks, and started dropping down. Squeak said, "Relax, Doc," and we sideslipped back and forth down the slot. There seemed to be about a foot clearance from the wing tips to the spruce trees on either side, but he set the little plane down with the skis right in the cat tracks.

We walked into the settlement: I saw what patients there were, we had coffee with the RCMP boys, then went out the way we came in.

Back in Yellowknife that night there was a little party at the Associated Airways shop for one of the pilots, Smoky Gray, who was leaving to take a job flying for one of the oil companies. Earlier in the winter Smoky was commended for a rescue he carried out when an ice floe broke off and carried a group of Native fishermen and their dogs out into the middle of Great Slave Lake. Smoky landed a Beaver with skis on the floating ice, picked off the fishermen and their dogs, and took off again, doubtless saving the lives of all concerned. The fact that he risked his own neck was all in a day's work. This was a way of life for those boys. Unfortunately, a week after the party Smoky flew into a hill in bad weather and was killed.

I talked to one of the guys a few years after I was at Fort Rae and he reported that of the pilots that I knew there, five of them had since got killed. I have never wanted to learn to fly a small plane. I think I could crash-land a plane if the pilot had a sudden heart attack or such, but I would just as soon not have to try it.

On a trip to Fort Rae from Yellowknife with Dave Floyd in a Norseman, I had the most uncomfortable experience. We were flying along at about 3,000 feet when I felt the worst sensation I have ever had, like my pockets were filled with rocks and we were being dragged down out of the air. Dave saw the look on my face and casually mentioned that we were picking up ice and would have to get out over the lake. We did a careful turn and soon were out above the lake ice. He dropped us down to 300 feet and we followed the shore ice all the way around to Fort Rae. If we stayed at that altitude the ice did not build up, but if we tried to go higher we felt it right away.

(I remember one time, many years later in the Cariboo country, flying with a pilot I had never flown with before, in weather that we never should have been up in. We were flying just above the treetops when we picked up some ice. The pilot asked, "Do you mind if I smoke, Doc? When you see me chewing it you'll know I'm really getting nervous." I said, "I don't care if you are smoking it, chewing it, or sticking it up your ass; just fly this goddamn thing." I was *not* relaxed.)

Back in Fort Rae, a message came in on the HBC two-way radio that there were some very sick people over at Fort Wrigley, down the Mackenzie River quite a few miles below Fort Simpson. A plane was to come in and pick me up, we would fly over to Fort Simpson and pick up the doctor there, and the two of us would go to Fort Wrigley and look after the emergencies. We picked up the doc at Fort Simpson and I was glad to see he was a classmate of mine—Eric from U of A medical school and a good fellow.

On that January day there were four feet of ice on the Mackenzie River, so we didn't have to worry about the plane breaking through. We climbed up the riverbank to the settlement, where we enjoyed a cup of coffee at the HBC trader's house after our long flight. The HBC man then took us through the dark night to the house where the patients were gathered. One of the patients had bronchopneumonia complicating measles; there were a few others with coughs, throat infections, and so on. We treated them on the spot. It was such a pleasure having another doctor to confer and work with. We both enjoyed it.

One kid was obviously the sickest. Eric and I checked him over together and we both independently diagnosed rheumatic fever with pancarditis (inflammation of the heart)—a pretty fancy diagnosis for a couple of young medics to make with only our eyes, ears, and stethoscopes. We both agreed that he had better get out to Edmonton where they had cardiologists, electrocardiogram equipment, lots of backup, and some talent and more expertise than we had.

I would take the sickest kid back to Yellowknife and put him on a plane to Edmonton. Eric would take the one with pneumonia to his hospital for treatment. There was a young Native woman who wanted to go to Fort Providence to work, so in the morning we bundled them all up in the Beaver and took off. Eric and I both had a snooze on board as we had worked late into the night. We flew up the Mackenzie River to Fort Simpson, where Eric got his patient on a dogsled for the hospital. We took off again and headed for Fort Providence, where we dropped off our one healthy passenger, then without further delay flew to Yellowknife. We got the sick young patient on the Canadian Pacific flight to Edmonton, having radioed ahead to the Camsell Hospital to meet the plane. I checked later and heard that the patient was doing well.

The early summer passed quickly, and at the end of June it was time for me to leave—to "go outside"—on to Montreal, New York, and the high-powered life of academic medicine. I left as quickly and quietly as I could. That north country and its people grow on you. I was not anxious to say my good-byes, but I had things to do. On the Canadian Pacific flight out we circled once and then headed south.

I flew to Edmonton, then Vancouver, visited with my brother Art and family, saw my mother, went over to Victoria where I proposed to my girlfriend, with whom I had corresponded while in the north. Then I took off for Montreal to start my year as senior intern in surgery at Queen Mary Veterans Hospital.

This was a very busy hospital looking after not only recently returned veterans, but current military personnel as well. Our consultants and active teaching staff were great. I volunteered for a three-month stint as neurosurgery resident as they did not have one and asked for volunteers. I did not have aspirations of becoming a brain surgeon, but knew I would be seeing lots of trauma where I hoped to practise. I thought it would be good to get some experience with head injuries. The chief of neurosurgery gave me lots of responsibility and taught me a lot. Also on our consulting staff were men from the Montreal Neurological Institute, including Willie Cone and the renowned Wilder Penfield.

As part of my job I presented problem cases to Dr. Penfield every Friday afternoon at Ward Rounds. That was an experience I will not forget. My presentations were not so great, but Dr. Penfield's discussions were certainly interesting.

I also enjoyed my rotation through plastic and reconstructive surgery. The consultants here, especially Dr. Fred Woolhouse, were fantastic. I learned stuff from Dr. Woolhouse and the plastic and reconstructive surgery staff, as well as from the neurosurgery staff, that I used in surgical practice over the next 40 years.

My girlfriend came to Montreal and we were married in September of 1953.

I had joined the RCAMC reserve in Victoria while at the Jubilee Hospital, and in Montreal I transferred from the 13th Field Ambulance to the 12th Field Ambulance. In the winter it was great sport doing ski manoeuvres in the Laurentian Mountains, getting captain's pay ($18 per day) and enjoying myself while doing it.

After a year at Queen Mary's I spent a year at the Montreal Children's Hospital—pleasant and worthwhile. Kids get sick fast and get better fast. Most of the medical staff were bilingual and good guys. Both medical staff and nursing staff were dedicated, so we had a great esprit de corps.

## A Fight a Day

Our next move was to the Big Apple and the Columbia University First Surgical Division at Bellevue Hospital Medical Centre in New York City. Bellevue Hospital had 5,000 beds and was an amazing place, just off Lower Manhattan, close to the Bowery. We had the wildest, weirdest clientele you could imagine.

Four medical schools worked and taught at Bellevue. I was affiliated with Columbia University. Then there was Cornell University, which taught also at New York Hospital, a few blocks away; New York University Medical School; and New York Postgraduate School. The logistics, one would think, would be unmanageable, but things seemed to run smoothly enough. All services supplied interns and junior residents to the emergency department, which operated 24 hours a day and averaged an ambulance unloading every four minutes. We had an armed guard carrying a nightstick and a .45 calibre revolver patrolling the main entrance area to protect the staff from street gangs.

I averaged a fight a day of some kind while living in New York. Hispanic and Black citizens were constantly having gang wars. The Hispanics, being smaller and weaker, usually resorted to knives, so that gave us great experience in dealing with stab wounds of all kinds.

Women had their own favourite methods of revenge. Jealous wives or girlfriends doused the guilty male's testicles with a bottle of nitric acid. We found that the skin of the testicles had great powers of regeneration and healed amazingly well with very conservative management.

Teaching New York boys to treat *anything* conservatively was difficult. Since the hospital was a completely charitable institution and it was known that we did a lot of good work, there were always free tickets for us to all the Broadway shows, the Metropolitan Opera, and other entertainment. I used to enjoy the emergency room. Among other things, only working eight-hour shifts gave us a little more free time. And we were completely on our own; while we did not get much actual teaching there, we had a chance to develop techniques of our own that came in handy later.

Weekly surgical grand rounds were a learning experience, I'll tell you. Every week at Bellevue we had a variety of cases that you would see in few places. And somebody on the consulting staff always had seen such a case before. Such a variety of expertise was present that you couldn't help learning if you kept your ears open.

Living in New York City was an experience all its own. New Yorkers showed a mixture of sophistication and primitive savagery that was hard to imagine. We had a house staff, residents and interns, of 400 doctors from 75 countries around the world. Our consulting staff included renowned specialists in every field you could name. We worked our way through a phenomenal amount and variety of surgery. I was a senior assistant resident, learning from the two chief residents, who were very knowledgeable and who worked under the guidance of a wide selection of specialist consultants. At Bellevue the resident staff did almost all the actual surgery, except for some exceptionally rare and complicated cases for which they would invite a recognized expert in the field who would show us all how to do it. The chief residents performed some of the more heavyweight surgery, with help from the assistant residents. A consultant scrubbed in to direct the procedure and keep us all out of trouble.

Sometime after the middle of the year the chief resident and the chief of surgery called me into the office. They asked me if I would be interested in staying on for another year and a half—half a year more as assistant resident, then half a year as second chief resident, and the last half year as first chief resident.

Needless to say, I was speechless, but ultimately I had to turn it down. As assistant resident I was still only getting $120 per month and I didn't think that was going to change. I had been offered the chief residency, at $300 per month, in Calgary, and my wife would be able to resume nursing back in Canada, so we could afford to live.

I sadly told the men at Bellevue that I could not accept the offer, even though I would like to. This was the first time that I really resented being poor. I should add that not only was I poor, but also dumb. I am sure that the chief of surgery at Bellevue could have used his influence to help us, but I was too stupid to ask him. I also did not know how bad a medical town Calgary was at that time. I was not unhappy to leave New York, but I could have stood it for a year or two longer.

When the year was up we packed our belongings in the old Buick car that we had bought and headed across the George Washington Bridge, through New Jersey, onto the Pennsylvania Turnpike, and west across the continent to Vancouver, B.C. We visited in Vancouver for a few days, then crossed back into the U.S. to keep from paying duty on our car, and officially re-entered Canada two weeks later when our minimum time out of the country was accepted. We drove up through the Kootenays, then to Banff, and into Calgary.

I didn't know anybody much in Calgary, but I knew of a few people there. I started work at the military hospital and soon found out what a bad move I had made. The hospital was not set up for teaching, period. This, my final year of training, should have been taken up with advanced surgical experience. Instead I spent most of my time teaching the junior residents to do hernia repairs and the occasional appendectomy. Big deal! Our staff surgical rounds weren't worth going to, and it was not for lack of effort on my part.

I also found out that there were more iniquitous practices going on, like fee splitting. Old-time GPs referred their surgery to old-time surgical buddies instead of to the best and most qualified young surgeons in the city. I'd heard about these things in medical school, but I never really thought that they actually happened.

I had a slight notion of practising in Calgary when I finished training, but after I talked to various people and found what a hard time some of the newly trained surgeons were having trying to get a start, I decided to hell with that idea. In the spring of 1957, while I was still at Calgary, I wrote my speciality exams. I passed the written exams but blew the orals. I just hadn't had the surgical experience in that last year to do a good oral exam. We had to eat, and there was no point in staying in Calgary. I instinctively looked towards the Cariboo, my home, where I had friends. I already had my B.C. licence to practise, so we pointed the old Buick west through Banff and Golden, over the Big Bend highway, which was a terrible road then, to Kamloops, Cache Creek, and up to Quesnel.

## Troubles on the Home Front

In 1957 I made arrangements with a Quesnel building contractor and property owner to fix me up an office in what had been Overwaitea's feed and flour warehouse. I became acquainted with the fellows already in practice in the town and soon found out that I was not welcome—unless, that is, I wanted to work for them.

A young Japanese-Canadian doctor from the University of Alberta, who had worked with me in Calgary, came out to Quesnel at the same time I did, and the doctors at the existing clinic up the street gave him the same type of welcome I got. They refused to give us anaesthetics for surgery, they made themselves pretty obnoxious, especially their senior man, and their wives snubbed our wives.

I decided, "This is the place I want to work and to hell with those guys." They couldn't keep me from getting hospital privileges, and both the other young fellow and I started to work.

He had an added problem, however—racism within the established medical community. Although he and his pleasant wife were both good people, it was tough for them, trying to buck racial intolerance as well as the other problems we had. They stayed for six weeks and packed it in. They went back to Southern Alberta and we lost a good man.

I was better off than he was in that I had a few old friends in Quesnel to give me support. When I first arrived in Quesnel, with no money of course, I needed some cash for groceries and house rent. I went down to see Ray Commons, manager of the Royal Bank. He agreed to loan me $1,500. I found out later that theatre owner and real estate investor Paul Gauthier had backed my loan. I had no collateral and I think Ray wondered if he would ever see the money. Three months later he loaned me another $2,500 to keep me going. But by that time I was on my way.

Many years later Ray Commons fell and broke his hip in Quesnel. I had the great pleasure of fixing it for him, putting a pin in it with a satisfactory result. I was grateful to get the opportunity to do something for him, and I told him that. We decided we were about even. He was able to walk again in a very short time.

I also had surgical friends in Kamloops, particularly Dr. Jim Rankine in Kelowna, who was an excellent and well-respected surgeon. Many of my patients who strayed into his office he sent straight back to me, with a good word on my behalf.

I talked to the registrar of the B.C. College of Physicians and Surgeons. He was sympathetic, but told me the College could not force the other group to co-operate with me. If it was an emergency case where I needed help, such as an anaesthetic, and they refused to help, then they could be charged with negligence or some other charge under the Medical Act. The registrar told me to just carry on and keep my nose clean, then talked about his own troubles as a young doctor. In his first practice in a small town in Manitoba, an old doctor was giving him a bad time. Soon after, the registrar-to-be had the distinct pleasure of attending this old doctor's funeral. The registrar said, "Maybe you might be just as lucky."

So I carried on and looked after my patients, and the patient load grew every week. The patients would see me, then go to the city and get the same diagnosis I had given earlier. Then they would come back to me for treatment. I even encouraged them to get a second opinion. After quite a few patients followed that routine, returning to me for treatment, I got pretty busy.

The first day at work I told the receptionist that no one should ever be turned away from our office because of lack of money to pay. I did a lot of free work in those days prior to Medicare, but I still paid off Ray Common's loan in good time.

There was a flu epidemic that spring; I recall making sixteen house calls on what was supposed to be my day off. I was in the operating room by day and making calls at night.

I hired a young Chinese doctor who had just completed a year of anaesthetic training at Dalhousie. That helped some, but it wasn't working out well and finally we decided that George had better try it someplace else, perhaps in Vancouver's Chinatown. He left and took with him the best-looking blonde secretary we had in the hospital office. George was last seen driving a pink Buick convertible on Vancouver's West Pender Street.

Dr. Bill Matheson, who was working up in Wells, 60 miles east of Quesnel, knew of my troubles. I think he had also had some dealings with the guys up the street, so he volunteered to come down and give anaesthetics for me. He would catch a ride down on a freight truck with

Bill Kelly at 7 a.m., we would operate all morning, and he would catch the truck back up after lunch.

Prior to Dr. Bill's help, I would administer the anaesthetic myself, usually a spinal if it was for abdominal cases or on a lower extremity, and one OR nurse would watch the patient while the other assisted me with surgery. If we were doing tonsils, of which there were quite a few cases, I would induce the anaesthetic with chloroform, which was faster. When the patient was asleep we would switch to ether, and the nurse would drip either while I snicked out the tonsils and adenoids. I would not do tonsils again that way for any money. Our nurses were really good and we had little trouble and no fatalities. The nursing staff was all very supportive and remained that way even when things got better. I am eternally grateful to them all.

I used to get a chance to help Dr. Bill in Wells once in awhile, and every time I could help him out I did. We did the last major surgery performed in the old Cariboo Gold Quartz Hospital in Wells. Bill phoned me about midnight and told me he had admitted a woman to hospital that night who was having severe abdominal pain, which was getting worse. Because of the poor co-operation we got from the guys at Quesnel, Dr. Bill and I decided that I should go up and see her there. My wife came with me because I did not like to drive on crooked roads before operating: holding the wheel made my hands stiff. I examined the patient and made a diagnosis of acute torsion of a right ovarian cyst.

The nurses set up the operating room and I was glad to see it was well equipped. Bill gave the patient a spinal anaesthetic, and the matron assisted me with surgery. Another woman was instrument nurse. I made a low transverse incision to gain access to the pelvis. A rapid exploration showed that she did indeed have a torsion of a moderate-sized ovarian cyst that was gangrenous. She also, to my surprise, had a two-month pregnancy in her uterus, which I had not felt when I examined her before the operation.

She admitted that her cycle had been irregular, but she said she had not skipped any. With as little manhandling as I could, I quickly cross-clamped the ovarian pedicle and removed the gangrenous, twisted, cystic ovary. We ligated the pedicle, did a quick exploration of the abdominal contents, ligated any bleeding points, and then got out.

Blood loss was minimal and we produced very little operative trauma. We closed the abdomen carefully but without wasting time. Bill reported that everything was quite stable, so we transferred her back to bed, where she would be watched over by the nurses. I thanked the nurses for their help and had a cup of hospital coffee with Bill, following which my wife and I got in the car and drove back to Quesnel. The post-op progress was unremarkable, and six to seven months later, at term, the woman delivered healthy twin girls.

I was getting busier and not only needed another doctor to give anaesthetics, but also to help with the general caseload. Dr. Doug Lahay was a young doctor working in Ashcroft, and he wrote me a letter saying he'd like to come to help me out. I offered him a full partnership, so up he came with his wife and family. That made life much better. Doug was a good general practitioner, not afraid of work, quite astute, with a special interest in anaesthesia. This suited me just right. After a few years Doug moved to Vancouver, where he subsequently became a full-time anaesthesiologist at UBC.

## Silencing the Cowboy Crooners

In the meantime we had a lot of fun and did a lot of work. In early days in Quesnel we had a radio station, but the station was not too flush and on occasion it sold radio time to citizens who provided their own program.

One of these home-grown productions was funded by Owens Department Store and featured the two young Chinese Owens boys singing cowboy songs, accompanied by themselves on guitar. Sometimes their old man joined in on a three-stringed Chinese violin. It was bloody awful.

We had some respite, though, when one of the boys broke his wrist. Doug Lahay gave him a shot of anaesthetic while I manipulated the fracture. I put on a cast from his armpit to his fingertips. Doug remarked that it was a pretty long cast for a small fracture.

I told him, "Shut up and look after your anaesthetic. We are going to have some peace and quiet on Sunday mornings for awhile around here."

One night we were finished a case in the operating room about midnight when Doug was on call. About that time a call came for him from a woman who thought she had pneumonia and wanted Doug to go see her at Brotherston's Cabins in West Quesnel. Doug changed into his street clothes and made the call.

The next day he told me that when he got there the door was locked, but there was a light on in a back window. He went around, looked in the window, and saw a man in bed with the woman. He yelled, "Open the goddamned door." They all went back to the bedroom, where he listened to her chest with his stethoscope, then turned her over his knee, pulled up her nightgown, and gave her a good shot of penicillin while her paramour looked on. Doug told me, "Damnit, if I go out in the middle of the night to see somebody with pneumonia, somebody is going to get a shot of penicillin in the ass."

## Getting a Hang of the P.R. Business

The RCMP had to have their lockup prisoners certified "Free from putrid and infectious disease" before they could be sent out to jail. The other doctors did not want to associate with such unsavoury characters, so they gave very poor service for this work. My old friend Jed Campbell told the sergeant that he was sure I would do this for them. He was right. Since my office was right downtown, I could slip out across the alley for them and check a couple of jailbirds between other cases, and they were happy as anything with the quick service. It didn't take long before it all added up. From that beginning I gained most of the policemen and their families for patients. The federal government covered their medical expenses.

When examining females I *always* had a nurse in with me to make the patients feel more comfortable. Word spread of this practice, and our office developed a steady run of young maternity patients.

I hand-picked my staff in the beginning so that I didn't have to tell them to be nice to people. I found it interesting that a smart woman with common sense did not have to have medical or nurse's training to be able to tell on the phone which were urgent cases and which were just pushy.

A number of my old friends started coming in as patients after they found out that I was not a threat to their health. Doug Lahay and I were getting more than we could handle, so we got a third man, Dr. Bill McIntyre, to help us. Bill was a logger from Lumby in his college days and fitted in just great in the Cariboo. He was also very astute, and his wife Stella was a nice person.

Shortly after Bill came we added another man, John Maile, from London, England. John had a year of anaesthesia training in Vancouver, which was advantageous.

Since I wanted to get more into surgery, I had to get back east and into the academic scene so that I could write and pass my surgical specialist exams. I had all the practical operative experience but needed more academic background to hold my own with the oral exam guys. After six years of work I had saved enough money to get away, so I hired a smart young fellow, Gordon McGee, to fill in for me and I took off for Montreal.

## Special Fellow from the Boondocks

I left my family in Quesnel, got a little housekeeping apartment across from the Medical Library at McGill University, and enrolled in the

Montreal General Diploma course in surgery, where I knew most of our teachers. With the reading lists they gave us each week I immersed myself in the depths of the library and became a serious student of advanced surgical practice.

I studied from morning until night and even got to the stage where I had coffee breaks with the library staff. I also got a job as a lab instructor in the anatomy department at McGill, along with two other fellowship candidates. We spent Tuesday and Thursday mornings in the lab demonstrating anatomic structures to the medical students: a good learning experience for all of us. I remarked to the department head one day that they were a keen bunch of students, and he replied that they should be, there were six PhDs in the class.

In the summer, the diploma course in surgery wound up and the speciality written exams were held. I think all of us passed them. Then we had free time from July until the orals were held in Montreal in early December.

I had attended a surgery seminar at the Cleveland Clinic before I started the diploma course, and there I met the chief of surgery, Dr. Stanley Hoerr. I told him of my program and that I would be going back to the frontier to practise general surgery. I said I knew the Cleveland programs were filled for the year, many for a four-year program, but I asked if it would be possible for me to go down at my own expense and just observe what they were doing in the operating rooms and attend their conferences.

He was quite interested in my work out in the boondocks and told me that when I was finished in Montreal I should come down to Cleveland and he would enrol me there as a special fellow. They often had such surgeons from various parts of the world studying with them. I reported to the Cleveland Clinic and was promptly enrolled as a special fellow, sponsored by Dr. Hoerr.

I scrubbed every morning in the OR with the various surgeons, all excellent teachers, who explained to me, along with their regular fellows, all the finer points of what they were doing. Besides that, I was free to use the clinic library and video library as well as attend all the various conferences, which went on from 7 a.m. until 11 p.m. I never thought it was possible to absorb so much learning in so short a time.

The Cleveland Clinic surgeons were all outstanding in their fields and all great guys to know. Dr. Rupert Turnbull in abdominal surgery and Dr. George Crile Jr. who, like his father, was renowned in head and neck surgery as well as in upper abdominal surgery, were absolutely great teachers. I enjoyed my time at Cleveland.

*I was elected president of the B.C. Surgical Society in 1981. I'm holding the "talking stick," which is a symbol of authority in the society's meetings.*

In 1981, when I became president of the of B.C. Surgical Society for a year, I had the pleasure of inviting Dr. Robert Hermann, the current chief of general surgery at Cleveland, to be our guest speaker, an invitation he accepted.

I went from Cleveland to Montreal for the oral exams, and this time I had no problem. On my return to Quesnel I could now practise surgery with the initials FRCS(C) as well as FACS behind my name.

In addition to adding John Maile, I made a recruiting trip to Britain and signed up Dr. Peter Calder from the wilds of Scotland to come over and work at the Holley Clinic. Peter was qualified in both internal medicine and neurology in Britain and was a good addition to the clinic. Dr. Gordon McGee, the UBC graduate who had been filling in for me, went to the U.S. and did training in internal medicine and hematology at Cook County Hospital in Chicago. He would have come back and joined us at the Holley Clinic, but there was already an internist in town at the other clinic, the Avery, and he thought two would be more than we needed, so he went to Terrace. I wish we could have kept him because, as it turned out, only a few months after going to Terrace he was walking down the street when he was struck by a drunk driver and killed. A terrible loss of talent and of a good friend.

We took on three or four other doctors from Britain who were with us for variable periods of time, but they could not be classed as assets. We did add an ENT man from Edinburgh who was a good man and is still with the clinic. We carried on with six or seven doctors as a small but active clinic.

After the head man from up the street left town, tensions between the two medical groups eased somewhat. We weren't all real buddy-buddy, but we did act a little more civilized.

# TEN

# B.C.'s First Intensive Care Unit

On a visit back to the Cleveland Clinic I picked up the idea of starting an Intensive Care Unit. Not a single hospital in British Columbia, including Vancouver General Hospital or St. Paul's, had an ICU. I believed that we could use a vastly scaled-down version of such a unit for our serious surgical post-op cases as well as head injuries, multiple traumas, or other serious cases.

At that time hospitals used special nurses in private rooms instead of ICUs. These special nurses were often older people who had trouble handling a busy shift on the ward, so opted to take a special case where they didn't have so much galloping around to do. These old girls were all right and were great knitters, but the system seemed backwards to me. Here we had our most demanding cases, with lots of gadgets to look after, being handled by staff members who were just about ready for retirement.

The situation at Cleveland, with its high-tech procedures, was a far cry from what we had, but it seemed reasonable to have a small unit close to the nursing station, where we would have our brightest and most energetic young nurses on staff. That way extra help would be available if needed. We would treat our most demanding cases here until they were over the critical phase, and they could then be transferred to a general ward.

I heard that they did have an Intensive Care Unit at the Royal Alexandra Hospital in Edmonton, where I had been an intern once, so I made a quick trip over there to see it. That unit was pretty big and fancy, with lots of monitoring equipment, but the basics were the same as those I wanted to install. The hospital administrator was Dr. George Allin, a classmate of mine, so he gave me the full tour. They were very proud of their unit.

Before going further I must voice my appreciation for the full co-operation given me by the late Mrs. Inez McCall, our director of nursing at that time. She and her full nursing staff, as well as the hospital administration, were supportive of our venture, which entailed quite a bit of specialized training for the nurses working in the new unit. The medical staff volunteered to teach and the nursing staff volunteered to learn on their own time. These nurses learned cardio-pulmonary resuscitation, which was not as common then as it is now; endotracheal intubation, which the anaesthetists taught them every day in the operating room; the fine points of the Glasgow coma scale, important in trauma cases as well as for other unconscious patients; and how to quickly establish a mainline IV for rapid restoration of blood volume. They became proficient at operating monitoring equipment, which is part of the everyday operation of a present-day ICU. I think the internists were quite surprised at how well they read ECGs.

It wasn't too much later that ICUs became established in most of the hospitals throughout the province and the country as a whole. Here in our hospital, as in many others, these units were pre-empted by the cardiologists due to the fact that much of the high-tech equipment was designed for monitoring cardiac cases. But let us not forget that it was a surgeon who brought home the concept and got it organized.

Our unit consisted of four beds with monitors, central suction, wall oxygen outlets, and a mobile cart (crash cart), which was stocked with all emergency drugs and equipment and with a daily roster of staff to operate it. This cart was on wheels and could be taken immediately to wherever in the hospital it was needed. Our ICU has proved invaluable since the first day we started it up. I shudder to think of the day when some bureaucrat from Victoria makes the decision that the people out here in the boondocks don't deserve or warrant such fancy equipment.

## Half-Way Measures Will Not Do

The late Dwayne Witte was in for a check-up when I told him that I was a medical consultant, not a preacher, but that I would seriously recommend that he stop smoking and drinking if he wanted to live very long. Half-way measures would not do. He wondered if he could wait until after the Big Creek Stampede, which was coming up shortly and which we both attended. A few weeks later I had to phone Marion Witte about something and I asked how Dwayne was. He was in the other room and I heard her yell at him, "Hey, Dwayne, Doc wants to know how you are doing." In a minute she passed on the reply, "Tell him I quit smoking and drinking— but I still lie a lot." Dwayne was a great guy and a generous friend, with his old black hat and a pair of leather riding cuffs that he seldom took off. He made his decision as to how he wanted to live and for how long; I didn't argue with him and he didn't last long.

I had some medical friends in the city who were confident enough of their abilities that they did not have to worry about competition from the frontier. They were always willing to give me advice and help when we were stuck with a case in our community hospital and could not get the patient airlifted out. In the case of acute head injuries, we had about one hour to get victims into the OR from the time their pupil started to dilate until we got them decompressed and the intracranial bleeding stopped. Not infrequently I did the emergency care, and Dr. Gordon Thompson, chief of neurosurgery at VGH, was always available for consultation— only as far away as the phone. There was no point in arranging road or air ambulance in dicey weather if the patient was going to be dead on arrival. I made no pretence of being a brain surgeon, but if the case was urgent and time was of the essence, I did not mind "going for it."

Another good friend was orthopedic surgeon Fergus Ducharme at the Regional Hospital at Prince George, who was always glad to give me advice. Fergus had been on the consulting staff at the University Hospital in Ottawa and was well trained and experienced.

My experience in the field of vascular surgery was not extensive when I came to Quesnel. In training I had concentrated on things I expected to do more often. But here, if we were able to control the bleeding without further damaging the artery, I was always assured of help from Dr. Joe Sladen, senior vascular surgeon at St. Paul's Hospital in Vancouver. If a case required further grafting or revision, I could send the patient down and Joe would do whatever else needed doing, without unkind comments about what should or should not have been done. If patients quibbled, they would be reminded that if the treatment had not been done in a timely manner they would probably not have a limb to show for it.

I had the added advantage of having some experience with acute head injuries due to my three-month residency in neurosurgery when I was at Queen Mary Veterans Hosptial in Montreal. At times during the residency I was almost out of my depth, like the day I was helping our staff neurosurgeon do a craniotomy on a cop shortly after I started on the service. This was a real great neurosurgeon and good teacher, but absent-minded. We finished the case and without further adieu he took off his gloves and mask and said, "You can close, Dr. Holley," and walked out. It was the first craniotomy I had ever seen and I knew nothing of proper closure of the various layers. But the OR scrub nurses knew all about it and showed me the whole routine. You know, if you don't act too superior and are not afraid to ask, it is amazing how much you can learn from the people you work with. Forty years later I am still learning that.

## A Quick Coffee in Vancouver

One night in the early winter the duty doctor in emergency called me in to the hospital to see a highway accident victim. This fellow and his wife were coming from Prince George to Quesnel when they hit the rear end of a flatdeck truck parked on the highway. It was snowing and the road was slippery. This fellow complained of discomfort in his left upper ribs, but it was the severe pain across his upper back that bothered him most. X-rays showed nothing, but the duty doctor was perplexed because every time they tried to stand him up he went flat on them. His wife in the passenger seat was uninjured.

When I saw him he was conscious, sober, with no alcohol on his breath. His pupils were normal and he had no clinical evidence of fractures or chest or belly injuries. His X-rays of upper and lower spine were rechecked and looked normal. But his upper back continued to hurt, all the way across. I checked his blood pressure and it was high in both arms at 186. His femoral pulses in both lower limbs were barely perceptible. These few but important findings indicated to me that he had a partial rupture of his thoracic aorta. He had been wearing a seatbelt, we believed, and that fact also suggested a deceleration injury to his upper aorta. If the aortic rupture had been complete he would only have survived three or four minutes. But if the few shreds of fibrous adventitial tissue held on until we could get him to a centre equipped for cardiothoracic surgery, the surgeons could put him on a pump and replace the damaged segment of aorta with a teflon graft and he would be okay. I phoned one of my cardiothoracic surgery friends, Al Guerien in Vancouver, and told him what we had. He said that if we could get the patient down there, they would look after him.

This was in the days before air-sea rescue was available, but the RCAF out of Comox used to do emergency flights for us from the frontier areas, so I phoned them. It was about nine o'clock on a Saturday night. The duty officer answered the phone and said that flying conditions around Hope were very bad, with icing, and they had no aircraft equipped for flying in that kind of weather. He added, however, that they would come up at 0800 hours in the morning, but if anything bad happened in the night "would I please let him know so they would not make the trip for nothing."

I told him thanks, that the patient's wife was sitting across the desk from me and his words were quite reassuring. Then I hung up. I thought, "You bastards are having a Saturday night party and that is why you haven't got anything ready to fly in that kind of weather."

I had to get some other means of transport. I thought of Heinz Wittenbacker, who flew West Fraser Timber's plane, based in Williams Lake. I phoned there, but got his baby-sitter, who told me he was at a party somewhere and she didn't know when he would be in. I phoned the

Vancouver Airport manager, told him what our problem was, and asked him if there was anyone around there that we could get to fly up. Our airport was cleared of snow and 737 jets had been landing regularly. He phoned back to say there was no one. I tried Calgary. I had flown in a corporate jet direct from Quesnel to Calgary and it took an hour and a quarter. The manager phoned back from the Calgary airport and he said yes, they had someone who would come, but they needed $1,000 up front. I said that would be fine and got him some credit references. I thought a man's life was worth that much—I had spent more for less and only got a hangover out of it. I thanked the manager at Calgary but asked him to wait just a little bit so I could try again to get someone closer. Meantime the clock was ticking and I knew our time was limited. It was getting later in the night. The patient was still stable, but I was sweating.

Then the phone rang. It was Heinz phoning from Williams Lake—he had just got in. I didn't even ask him if he was sober. Heinz said it would take him fifteen minutes to get to the airport there, half an hour to warm up and service the aircraft, and twenty minutes to get to Quesnel. The plane was a Cessna 421 turboprop, capable of flying high enough to get over the Coast Range, and Heinz was checked out for all-weather and night flying. I also knew that Heinz was a very good pilot. He told me when to have our patient at the airport and right on time the 421 came gliding in to the airport. We carefully loaded our patient onto a special stretcher, narrow enough to use on small aircraft.

His wife was with us, and Heinz said, "Yes, there's enough room for her on the plane." Then my Holley Clinic partner Dr. John Maile and I climbed aboard, armed with an endotracheal tube and ambu bag that we could use to intubate and breathe for him if necessary. John had the medications he would need if we had to anaesthetize the patient on the way. I brought a couple of chest tubes that I could use to decompress his chest if he started leaking blood or building up intrapleural pressure. We also had seven bottles of cross-matched blood and a good IV going. We knew that if his damaged aorta blew, it would be game over right now and our seven bottles of blood would be of no help. But if bleeding or pressure changes occurred more gradually we could cope with that. I just hoped the weather was not too bumpy if we had to put in a chest tube in flight.

Heinz revved her up and we took off, up and over the mountains, straight for the Vancouver airport. It was raining so hard when we came in to land that we couldn't see 30 feet ahead of us, and they brought us in for an instrument landing. Heinz brought the little plane in so smoothly that there wasn't even a bounce. An ambulance met us on the strip and we transferred our patient and his wife and our stuff and headed for St. Paul's Hospital. We were *very* careful in the transfer.

Al Guerien met us at the hospital and took delivery of our man. The patient had angiography to confirm the diagnosis and subsequently had resection of the damaged aorta and repair by teflon graft. Dr. Maile and I had coffee, and after seeing that the patient's wife was cared for we got a lift back to the airport from the ambulance crew. Our efficient pilot had the aircraft gassed up, serviced, and ready to go so we jumped in and headed back to Quesnel, thanked our pilot, and went home for Sunday morning breakfast.

My wife said to me, "What have you been doing all night?"

I told her, "Oh, John and I went down to Vancouver for coffee this morning." Three months later the patient was down from Prince George and dropped into the Holley Clinic to say Hello. I thank West Fraser who volunteered the use of their plane and pilot.

## On the Other Side of the Judge's Bench

During the summer of 1970 our place at Dragon Lake was being overrun with hippies and hoods of all kinds. It started when the rainbow trout were running up our creek the first part of May.

Native people were snagging spawners during the daytime to smoke or pickle; I didn't mind that so much, apart from empty wine bottles being scattered around the pasture where I had purebred colts and cattle running. But these other no-goods were coming in at night and clubbing fish and throwing them out on the creek bank to rot and stink. They were sneaking up the creek past my house to where the barn and machine sheds were located and were hijacking gas from my bulk tank for their vehicles.

One day I drove in to find a hippie having a bowel movement right on my lawn. I told him he had better get the hell out of there. He replied that he had to shit. I told him that if he didn't get off my lawn and get out of there I would kick his ass so hard he wouldn't be *able* to have a B.M. He went, reluctantly.

Another day I was hauling a calf home when I saw two guys lying flat in a furrow in my pasture. I got out of the truck, went over, and marched them over to the gate and out to the road. When they got off my property and set foot on the road they turned around and challenged me. They were fairly husky looking guys, about 30 years old.

They said to me, "Now what are you going to do?" with a smartass look on their faces.

I said, "Don't worry about what I am going to do, but what you had better do is to get the hell down this road and out of here." I went back to my rig and finished what I was doing. I then drove up to the house and phoned the RCMP. Two Mounties came out, and when I told them what direction the guys took, they went after them. The Mounties came back and told me they had given the two hoods a good talking-to. Big deal! They also recommended that I should not go down to the creek, especially at night, without a gun or a dog. I had my property well posted against trespassers.

One night at about one o'clock in the morning, after I had been operating half the night, I was awakened by a lot of whooping and hollering in the pasture down by the creek. After a half-hour of this racket I grabbed my old double-barrelled twelve-gauge, stuffed a handful of shells in my pocket, and went down to the creek. When I got to the top of the creek bank I hollered at them to get out of there. They ignored me and kept on yelling and screaming like idiots. I fired a volley over their heads and that got their attention. By this time I was in a corner of my corral and I could see shapes in the darkness coming over the opposite side of the corral. I told them to get the hell out of there and the shortest way was over the corral planks and out to the road. I could see the shapes of two cars parked on the road.

Three or four of them climbed over the fence and out, but I saw one shape peeling off to the left end of the corral and out a gate. I didn't know where he was heading, but it was not the shortest way out like he was told, and he could have got around behind me that way. I knew he was far enough away that I couldn't hurt him too much with the light number-seven birdshot I was using, so I blasted one out the gate. If he had headed for the fence and the road nothing would have happened to him, but if he pulled a move like trying to sneak around and get behind me, he might get some birdshot in his ass.

When the shot went off there was a hell of a commotion. He screamed and landed in the creek. The other guys screamed that they were going to kill me. I got my back up against the corner of the corral where they couldn't get in behind me, and I told them if they wanted to kill me to come right ahead—I had lots more shells. So they shut up, got their friend in the car, and took off at a high speed down the road.

At 8 a.m. two cops, not the ones I had recently complained to, arrived at the door saying that a man arrived in the hospital emergency department and said I shot him. I told them that yes, I had sprinkled a little birdshot in a hood's ass at 1 a.m. when he was terrorizing my place at Dragon Lake.

I guess the wires were pretty hot between the Quesnel RCMP detachment and the attorney-general's department in Victoria. Here was a well-known, respectable citizen protecting his property from being overrun, after requesting help from the police many times over the past several weeks. In the wisdom of the attorney-general, this citizen had to be charged with either shooting with intent to wound or dangerous use of a firearm. The maximum penalty ranged from four to seven years in jail.

One of the cops at Quesnel gave me a little tip when we were by ourselves. He told me that Lee Skip was the best lawyer around and that they usually got him for Crown counsel. The cop said that if he were me, he would get in touch with Lee right away and retain him as my lawyer. I did just that.

This case was drawing a lot of local attention among ranchers and others as ranchlands in the area were being overrun and fences cut by snowmobilers and four-wheelers. People were wondering when somebody was going to do something about it. About now I was wishing everybody would shoot their own goddamn trespassers.

The case was being tried by judge only. One of the local judges, whom I had known since my school days, disqualified himself. The other judge was a reasonable sort of man. He wasn't a bad bet for me because my partners were currently working hard on him, treating his narcolepsy, trying to keep him alert enough so that he could stay awake through a whole case and render a judgment at the end.

The day of judgment finally came. Witnesses were sworn in, the court reporter took her place, the judge sat down, all very formal. I was asked for a statement and I simply said that either the hoods and hippies were going to run that farm or I was, and I thought it had better be me. I went on to relate recent events and challenges and police involvement or lack thereof. The prosecutor then called my good friend Dr. Fred Konkin from the competition, the Avery Clinic, to tell them about the birdshot.

Fred was embarrassed to have to testify. He told of being called to the emergency department at 2 a.m. to see a patient who was said to have received a gunshot wound. He said that they had taken an X-ray that showed the shot. The Crown prosecutor asked him how many shot there were. Fred replied, "Approximately 140."

At that point Lee Skip leaned over and whispered to me, "What happened to the other ten?"

I whispered back, "It was dark." Lee Skip was an old upland bird hunter and knew, as I did, that there were 150 shot in a standard load of birdshot in a twelve-gauge shotgun shell. I really was not feeling very flippant at that time.

The case was eventually dismissed, much to my relief. I immediately had the four hoods charged with trespassing. They all skipped the country and went back to Northern Saskatchewan. The police apparently thought it was not worth the expense to bring them back for trial. By that time I had had enough court activity and had made my point, so was happy to let the matter drop. The whole show, with its attendant publicity, put an end to the night prowlers and people climbing through my fences and breaking down gates.

# ELEVEN

# Traumas and Cowboy Remedies

## Barn Calls

The two pharmacists at Spencer-Dickie Drugs did a pretty good business in veterinary supplies and, like me, liked animals. Between us we looked after quite a lot of animal welfare.

One Saturday a woman and her kids came into the drugstore with a little dog whose front leg was almost severed at the shoulder. It had got run over by a train. Alf Spencer phoned me to see if I would fix it. I said I would amputate it properly if he would give it an anaesthetic. He met me at the back door of the clinic, which was closed on Saturdays.

We took the dog into a spare room, Alf gave it continuous intermittent IV pentothal, and I trimmed up the mangled upper leg, actually doing an amputation through the shoulder joint. I trimmed and sutured the crushed muscle end together, repaired the shoulder joint, and tailored the skin flaps to make a smooth closure over the shoulder. We put a big protective dressing on and Alf let the dog wake up. He gave the woman some painkillers for the dog. We were quite proud of our job. The mother and kids were very happy and appreciative. The mother wanted to pay us, but we said we did it for the dog and the dog didn't have any money.

Next morning I phoned to see how the little dog was doing. The girl I talked to said that it was whining during the night so her dad took it out and shot it. We were somewhat teed off. We wished that if he was going to shoot the dog he would have done it before we spent all afternoon and $40 worth of supplies fixing it.

Another Saturday I got a call from my brother Bill on the dairy farm. He said he had a young cow that had been in labour for over three hours and was not progressing and he was going to try to do a Caesarean section on her. He wondered if I could scrounge up some instruments and suture material for him. He didn't actually ask me to do it for him, knowing this was supposed to be a day off. I gathered up what I needed and drove the twenty miles out to the dairy farm.

Bill was a good cowman, and if he could have got it out with a calf puller he would have. The cow needed a C-section all right, which he had seen the vets do before. But as he said, with the closest veterinarians at that time either 70 miles south in Williams Lake or 75 miles north in Prince George, by the time a vet got there it was too late.

We got the cow lying on clean straw in an empty stall. I gave her a series of paravertebral blocks with 2-percent Xylocaine local anaesthetic along the spine, blocking the spinal nerves for two spaces above and two spaces below (towards her tail) where I would make the incision. After clipping the hair we swabbed the skin with antiseptic solution and got to work. The cow lay quietly, relieved of pain by the regional block anaesthetic. I made a long incision in her right flank, opened the amniotic sac that contained the calf, and got a grip on the slippery little bugger. We pulled him out tail first and laid him on the clean hay.

He was a little slow to breathe, but after squeezing his chest a couple of times he gave a good breath in and was on his way and alive. We clamped and tied off the cord. We then sewed up the uterus with heavy catgut on a big curved needle. Prior to that we removed the buttons comprising the placenta, which a veterinarian friend has since told me you don't do. It was time-consuming work and I would gladly omit that part. By the time I stitched up the incision in the hide, my forearms were tired and my fingers were sore.

Both cow and calf survived and he sold them both that fall. The calf was mentally a little slow—from banging his head against the pelvic outlet for three hours, I guess. Bill's kids called the calf "Alex." I told Bill that I didn't mind doing a C-section on his cow, but I wished they wouldn't name the mentally impaired calf after me.

## Drunks, Young Punks, and Wheeler-Dealers

We had lots of trauma coming into the hospital, both industrial accidents and highway wrecks. In the 1950s and 60s the carnage off the highways around Christmas and New Year was ferocious. At one loggers' Christmas party, one of the men got run over and killed before he even got out of the company's yard.

One of the worst road disasters that I worked on was a two-car head-on collision on Highway 97 south of Quesnel, where seven people were killed.

I was at home after supper when I got called and went right out. The police were there and an ambulance had just arrived. Bodies scattered the road; several were children. Harold Hennigar, the ambulance operator, and I sorted them out as quickly as we could. The driver and his wife in one car were dead. The driver of the other car had both legs broken above the knees and was pretty shocky. Two little girls were lying on the road: one had a compound fracture of her jaw with her whole face torn open, bleeding. The other complained of belly pain and pain in her back. A woman had her face ripped open and a fractured lower jaw; she was unconscious, lying face up, and was gurgling away, choking on her own blood.

We flipped her over to let the blood drain out, then Harold ripped a seat out of the car, we laid her face down on this and carried her off to the side of the road. Harold got the man with the broken legs off the road and covered with blankets. We only had one ambulance, so we loaded the woman and the two girls and got them on their way to the hospital, eight miles away.

In the meantime I started sorting through the cars checking for victims. I found first one, then two, then three dead little kids huddled together in the back seat. They did not have a heartbeat or a spark of life among them. I thought I was pretty tough and hardened up to those kinds of things. Adults I can handle, but those poor little dead kids who didn't have a chance . . . It was no time to get holes in your armour. We had things to do, survivors to look after, but I didn't enjoy it.

The police car was parked on top of a rise a hundred yards or more above and north of the accident scene. The flashers could be seen for half a mile. A couple in a small Austin sedan was pulled over about level with the police car. Just as I was walking up the edge of the road to the police car I saw this sporty big car come roaring up the road, just flying; at the last moment the driver realized what he was seeing and slammed on his brakes—too late. The small English car flew in the air like a rocket. In midair the car burst into flames and then landed on all four wheels in the flat-bottomed ditch. All four doors flew open when it hit the ground, and at the same instant a body flew out each door. The woman on the passenger side clutched a baby. Both adults landed on their feet. The Mounties and bystanders put out the fire, and the police booked the driver who came speeding up and hit the Austin.

A bystander who had volunteered to help direct traffic was standing in front of the small car when it got hit. The front bumper hit the volunteer and knocked him head over heels, landing him on the pavement. I saw to him right away; he was conscious, got up, and walked to the edge of the highway. He said his back hurt pretty bad, so we got some blankets for him to lie on and some to cover him with, avoiding bending his spine. We would take him in with the next load when the ambulance got back.

I got the police to radio Emergency and call the other surgeon and some more doctors in to help us in the hospital. OR nurses were already on their way. When the ambulance came back and we had all the living victims on their way, I drove back to the hospital, formulating a plan of action.

When I got there the other doctors were busy checking over the victims. I took the little girl with the facial and lower jaw injuries to the OR first as she was still bleeding fairly badly. In the meantime I had the OR team prepping the woman with the ripped-up face and jaws. The other surgeon checked the girl with the belly and back injuries, and the lab cross-matched blood for the man with two fractured femurs and started an IV going on him. I had wired up the lower jaw fracture on the little girl and did as good a cosmetic skin closure as we could.

We were working on the woman, fixing her jaw and repairing her slashed face, when a nurse came by and said the volunteer fellow with the sore back was getting hard to arouse and his right pupil was dilated. I told her to get him into any available OR, shave his head, and have an anaesthetist intubate him. I controlled the bleeding on the woman and repaired what I could do as fast as possible, then prepared to go next door to look after what had suddenly become an intracranial haemorrhage—quickly fatal unless relieved. I would leave the woman's remaining repair job to the next surgeon to finish his earlier operation.

Before we even had time to cover up the operative field on the woman, however, another nurse came to say that the man had arrested and the anaesthetist was unable to resuscitate him. He had died, I am sure, of an extradural brain haemorrhage: quietly bleeding for one or two hours before suddenly showing acute symptoms, which were now irreversible. I felt extremely sorry for this man and his family—he tried to help out and got killed for it.

I was angry enough with those young punks who hit him that I could have clubbed them to death. I think they got fined $500 or some such slap on the knuckles.

The other patients—except for the driver with the fractured femurs, who went into shock and died—all made out fairly well. The young girl came back for follow-up for several years. Her parents were both killed and she and her sister lived with their grandmother. The woman with the facial injury went to the Coast later, where a plastic surgeon I knew did several reconstructive procedures to improve the fit of her broken jaw. When I last saw her she had some more work to do on her jaw, but the facial scars were not too bad and she was still attractive.

I thought of those little dead kids many nights over the years.

The highway accident that killed Dr. Donald Chalmers and his young wife, Janet, left the entire Holley Clinic sad. This couple and their three young children came over from Scotland, and Donald worked with us at the Holley Clinic. I used to make a point of telling all our doctors and other staff that they worked *with* us at the Holley Clinic, not *for* us. Donald had just received word that he had passed his Canadian exams, the Dominion Medical Councils, and was eligible to become a full partner in the clinic, starting on Monday.

He and Janet came out to our place for a barbecue on Sunday. They left in their small car about 5 p.m. Their children were with a baby-sitter. Part way into town Donald and Janet were hit head-on by a carload of partygoers in a big heavy Mercury sedan. Both were killed instantly, leaving three little kids completely alone in a strange country: no mother, father, nor any other close relatives. A cousin was located in Vancouver and the public trustee gave her custody of the children, with clearance to take them to their grandparents in Scotland.

On Monday afternoon the Insurance administrator phoned me from the B.C. Medical Association after hearing about the tragedy on the news. He told me that they had Donald's application for life insurance with the BCMA but that they could not process it because they didn't have his cheque for the premium. I asked him how much the premium was and he told me. I said, "It's in the mail," and he said, "Good! That's all we need, Al." Five minutes later it *was* in the mail. The kids got enough out of that to see them through secondary school.

A few weeks later the nice little house that Chalmers had bought was advertised to be sold by sealed tender through the government agent. I heard that a local young wheeler-dealer was bragging that he was going to buy it cheap and sell it at a good profit. I said to my wife, "Like hell he will!" I phoned my three partners and we borrowed some money, bought the house, sold it at a fair market value, and sent the money to the kids' grandparents, who we were sure would spend it on the kids' needs.

When the late Alex Fraser, B.C. minister of Highways, and his wife, Gertrude, went over to Britain a few years later, they looked up the Chalmers kids at their grandparents' home and they reported that the kids were doing well. Several years later, various members of the young family came over to visit Alex and Gertrude and the rest of us. The girl was married. One of the boys was an officer in the RAF, and I think the youngest boy was going to high school. We all did our best for them, but it didn't make up for the loss of their mother and father, who were well liked by everybody.

131

## Can't See Too Good

The Emergency Room was always good for a little humour, mixed in with the various disasters and tragedies.

One morning the ER nurse asked me if I would mind seeing a young kid who had got run over by a car. This ten-year-old boy looked a little scuffed up, but not seriously hurt. His mother, however, was carrying on something awful. She was weeping and wailing and saying, "That Leon! He tells me, 'Why don't you learn to drive?' But he never teach me. Now look what happens."

I said to the kid, "Where were you when you got run over?"

"Up on the back doorstep," he replied. The nurse and I both retreated around separate corners, where we stayed until we could contain ourselves.

One dark night two highway workers came in. One had a fractured tibia. They were grumbling and cussing away. They said that they were in a turnaround, not even on the highway, and were out of their vehicle, standing beside it, when this old truck left the highway and came right for them. One of them jumped straight up, out of the way, but the other one did not jump high enough and the old pickup's bumper got him on the legs.

After I finished looking after them, ordering X-rays of the tibia, etc., I went into the next cubicle to check this old couple that had got shook up in a car accident. The lady hastened to tell me that they were driving down the road, John was driving real careful like he always does, when all of a sudden a Highways truck came right across the road after them. I checked them both over and refrained from comment. A few minutes later when their daughter came in, her first words were, "I do wish Dad would stop driving."

On another case I tried to be a good guy and it almost backfired. This 75-year-old farmer, who lived with his bachelor brother just across the Quesnel River, was in for his driver's medical exam. When I did his exam I found that his eyesight was really not too good, but I thought, "Oh, hell, Carl only drives a mile or two in and out of town once a week, in second gear, to get groceries and farm supplies." I guessed I could slip him through.

I was driving downtown two days later and was starting through an intersection when I saw this old GM pickup bearing down on me. I floor-boarded her and just made it across with about a foot to spare or he would have nailed me. That taught me not to be so damned benevolent with some of these old-timers. The joke sure would have been on me.

## A Pig Makes a House Call

In between the various catastrophes, tragedies, and high-tech procedures, we seemed to have time for the occasional prank or party when things were quiet. With some of the friends I had, I didn't need enemies—like when my wife discovered a live pig turned loose in our living room.

I had solicited the help of some neighbour friends to help me bring home a piano. After we got it in from Jed's pickup truck, Jed Campbell, Buzz Heinzelman, Fred Kirsh, and I finished putting the piano in place and one of them remarked on what a nice big fireplace we had in our living room. He said, "It's big enough to roast a pig in."

I said, "You bring the pig, and we'll roast it." As soon as I said it I knew these were the wrong guys to give such a challenge.

Six months later, in mid-July, I came home from the operating room at one in the morning.

My wife told me, "Don't bother going to bed. Jed has a pig in his wife's car and he's bound to give it to you. He's had a few drinks." I agreed that he was unlikely to give up on the venture. Within a few minutes I heard this gawdawful commotion. Jed was at the back door, clutching a half-grown pig.

Mike, our big black lab, was trying to get it by the throat; our little wire-haired terrier was trying to screw it; and the pig was squealing bloody murder, all under a full moon and starlit sky.

In order to keep the neighbours from shooting us all, I told Jed to bring the pig and we'd have a drink. We barricaded the pig in the laundry room at the back door with kitchen chairs, where it settled down quietly. My brother-in-law was staying with us, so he got out of bed and joined us for a drink.

Jed and RCMP Sergeant John Stinson had been trying all summer to get a pig to bring us. They had come home covered with mud and pigshit many nights before Jed successfully ran this pig down on his way home from Prince George, scooped it up, tossed it in the trunk of the car, and kept on going.

After awhile we all said goodnight and went our separate ways to bed. The pig was quiet.

The first thing I saw in the morning was my wife standing in the bedroom doorway with a .22 repeating rifle in her hands, saying, "I don't know whether to shoot that damned pig or Jed Campbell. You should just see what the pig has done to our new dining room carpet." It had rooted things up quite a bit, but it wasn't irreparable.

Jed and his whole family, along with their car, were nowhere to be seen. Another neighbour told me they had gone to Beavermouth for the weekend. When my brother-in-law got back from morning goose shooting, he and I caught the pig and took it down in the basement where we shot it, skinned and dressed it out, and took it over to Campbells' outdoor barbecue. We invited Stinson and one or two others and had an nice pork barbecue. Stinson brought a bottle of Crown Royal that he had been given and we liberally basted the pork with it while it was roasting; the flavour was delicious.

## The Longest House Call

The longest house call I ever made up in the Cariboo was from Quesnel to Victoria and back. At midnight the phone rang; it was Gertrude Fraser. Gertrude and her husband, Alex, had lived in Saanich since Alex joined the provincial government cabinet as minister of Highways. Someone from the Victoria hospital had phoned her and she was genuinely concerned. Alex had spent a day in the hospital for observation, and the electrocardiographs showed that Alex's heart had stopped on several occasions—they wanted him back in hospital in the morning. But Alex signed himself out. He did not trust those city slicker doctors and she doubted if he would do what he was told. By this time of night he was in bed, sound asleep. What should she do?

He would have to have a pacemaker, that was for sure. We doubted that they would do the procedure in the middle of the night, even if he would let them. There was no point in waking him up, so I suggested that during the rest of the night perhaps she could sleep lightly. If she noticed any change in his breathing she should shake him awake and thump his chest a couple of times. I would be down there when it was light enough to fly in the morning.

I got a small plane out of Quesnel at first light and flew to Kamloops. There I caught the TransCanada DC8 to Vancouver and then a small plane to Victoria. I took a taxi from Pat Bay airport to the Frasers' house, where they were all up by now. Apparently Alex had had an uneventful night.

The family all worried about what to tell him. I solved that problem. Alex was an old truck driver as well as my old friend from the Cariboo country, so I talked to him in language that he understood. I said, "Listen you thick-headed old sonofabitch, you need a pacemaker and we are going in to the Jubilee to get it, and don't argue. Your heart stopped beating two or three times during the night when you had that recording cardiograph on, and we don't know when it will stop again." He didn't argue.

We got in the car with Gertrude and went straight to the hospital. We contacted the cardiologist, and I got hold of my old friend Jim Donald, who did thoracic surgery, and he said he would put the pacemaker in for us. I got into an OR suit and went into the OR with him to help keep Alex calmed down and relaxed during the procedure. All went well and he was adjusted to 72 beats per minute and felt well.

After Alex went home I went over to Premier Bill Bennett's office in the Parliament Buildings. He agreed to try and keep Alex's activities and workload toned down for a few weeks. I flew back home and went back to work.

The pacemaker was supposed to be good for six years. When five years were up I talked to Alex and told him that there was a great sale advertised on Taiwanese computers, pacemakers, and such gadgets and it would be a good time to get a new one. I said these ones were real cheap, but would be good enough for a politician. We had a constant ongoing discussion on how bad most doctors and most politicians were; however, we thought we were all right.

Art Lavington also had a pacemaker put in at the Coast after having some heart problem while hauling cattle. He came in to see me a month after he got back home. Cardiac problems were not in my line of work, but I saw him anyway. I think a lot of these old cowboys came to me because I talked their language. The doctors told him he should get in to see a doctor after he got back home, so here he was. Art said he thought the pacemaker must be working all right because he went out to run a bunch of cattle in off the big slide. That Fraser River bank was too rough to take a saddle horse on, so he rounded them up and ran them in on foot. I agreed that his heart must have been working pretty well.

## Cowboy Remedies

Some of those old-timers were tough. Paul Krestenuk was an interesting example. He had come over from Russia during the Bolshevik Revolution, making his way across Siberia and then getting on a boat to cross Bering Strait to Alaska. He worked his way inland, I don't know by what route, but he ended up in Cariboo country.

Paul started a trading post at the Carrier village of Nazko, 60 miles west of Quesnel. He traded with the Carrier for furs and built a store in which he sold groceries and dry goods. He ran a bunch of cows, using Native cowboys to help him. He cut hay on several wild meadows that he pre-empted. Paul also built a wagon road and winter sleigh road through the wild country to start another trading post at Kluskus Village, six days travel by team and sleigh from Nazko, with a crossing of the Blackwater River en route.

Paul pushed still farther: past Pan Phillips' Home Ranch, recrossing the Blackwater, past Eliguk Lake, to Ulkatcho Village to trade with the Ulkatcho, who ranged between there and Anahim. Not to be stopped, Paul even ran routes through Squinas Meadows, crossing the upper Dean River and going almost to the Rainbow Mountains in what is now Tweedsmuir Park. He traded all along the way. Having ridden and taken pack horses through that whole country from the Nazko Valley to Bella Coola, I can tell you that there is some rough country to travel through. Paul did a lot of the maintenance work on the old government road from Nazko to Quesnel in the early days.

One winter Paul had a very bad belly ache and was in the Quesnel hospital. Dr. Baker wanted to take his appendix out. After supper Paul saw a nurse go by with a big tray of instruments. He asked her, "What for those things?"

"That is for your operation," the nurse said.

"Get me my clothes."

"I can't do that."

"You show me where they are and I get them myself," Paul said.

He left the hospital, went down to Fraser's Freight Barn where his horses and sleigh were, harnessed and hitched up his four-horse team, and left town for his place at Nazko.

When Paul told me this story he asked me, "You know how I cur'em up those appendix? Olive oil and turpentine—I drink olive oil and I rub that sore belly with turpentine."

I haven't seen that method described in the New England Journal of Medicine or the Proceedings of the Mayo Clinic, but Paul's cure could well be found under alternative medicine because it sure was a different approach.

Paul was never enthusiastic about surgery, I discovered. Sergeant John Stinson and his RCMP boys brought Paul to the hospital in poor shape and severe pain, and we admitted him to Emergency with a big incarcerated hernia. In no way could I reduce the hernia. It was solidly stuck. We put him to bed, elevated his pelvis, applied an ice bag, and gave him 100 mg of Demerol to relax him. I told him we would leave it for a couple of hours and if it would not go back in we would have to operate, otherwise he would develop gangrene of the bowel and we would really be in trouble. He was pretty worried. I went back about an hour later, prepared to call the OR nurses.

When I went into his room, I smelled the distinct aroma of Scotch whisky; Paul wore a smile you could see a mile, and he asked for his clothes. A half bottle of White Horse Scotch stood on his bedside table. Harvey Denamy had been up to see him and left him a bottle of his favourite Scotch. I checked for his hernia and it was completely gone, and the whisky smell was coming from his belly, most noticeably in the area of his hernia.

Instead of drinking the Scotch, Paul used it to massage his hernia back in. He showed me how he had just massaged it over and over, pouring on more Scotch until it popped in. His pain was gone, he had a nice rest, and now he wanted to go home. I knew that big bulge was bothering him a lot before he came, and I would have liked to repair it while he was in. I could tell by the look on his face, however, that he meant it when he said he wanted out. The only way we could have kept him in would have been to forcibly restrain him, and I had no intention of doing that.

Stinson and his boys used to check on him whenever they were patrolling that way. About a year later he came to Emergency looking very ill and coughing. The duty doctor admitted him and he was eventually diagnosed with advanced tuberculosis. He died not long after. He made his living from the Native peoples and he died of their disease.

There were some other colourful Russians around Quesnel: Alex Loloff, Alex Bassoff, and Harry Gassoff. Loloff lived close to town, but I never knew much about him.

Alex Bassoff was one of the shiftiest looking old desperadoes you would see in a long time. He was a lean old cowboy, usually rode a good horse, and he slumped down in the saddle with his big black hat pulled down low so that his beady black eyes just peered out under the hat brim. He had a big, lean, slinky brown dog that followed along behind him.

Alex lived on Major Gook's farm at Dragon Lake for awhile, and we talked to him quite often. He had a habit when he was telling you something interesting of prefacing it with, "Honest-to-God, I tell you..." He had a homestead away out near the foot of Dragon Mountain and used to ride back and forth between there and Gook's farm. Richard Gook told me of the time he chanced to be in at Bassoff's place and recognized two of his family's axes in the woodshed. He accosted Alex about the axes and said he expected to get them back. Alex told him a long story about needing an axe to cut out a bunch of trees across the trail. Richard reminded him that there were two axes. Alex gave his usual spit on the ground and said, "Honest-to-God, I tell you, it happened twice."

Harry Gassoff, another colourful character, was a longtime friend of mine. Harry was from the Georgian Republic in the Caucasus Mountains of southern Russia. He had lived in Northern Saskatchewan, where he brought in carloads of broncs from Alberta, broke them to drive, and sold them to the Doukhobour farmers around Blaine Lake. He was a good horseman and also worked in the logging camps on the B.C. coast.

How he learned that my dad's stump ranch in the Cariboo was for sale, I don't know, but he arrived there in an old truck one day, bought the place, and brought his family. We became good friends when my wife and I moved back up to the Cariboo in 1957, and we became part of the Gassoffs' extended family. When I had personal problems of my own I did not see a psychologist or seek counselling from one of my confreres; I went out and talked to my old horse-trader friend, Harry Gassoff. Harry played the part of an old patriarch as his family grew to include sons and daughters-in-law, and grandchildren.

I have to admit that he was a real male chauvinist. He was a firm believer that woman's place was in the kitchen. His wife Rosie patiently suffered through his tirades. She recounted a terrible catastrophe to my wife one day. Harry had parked his new station wagon in the garage, with instructions for her not to touch it as she had an old Chevy to drive. She had to go to the store for something and her car wouldn't start, so she thought she would just take Harry's station wagon. She tiptoed into the room where he was sleeping on the sofa and slipped his car keys out of his pocket. She got in, started up the car, and started to back out. In order to see better behind her, Rosie opened the left front door just a little. But the wall studs stuck out too far and the door caught on one of them.

Rosie panicked and instead of putting her foot on the clutch, she pushed the gas pedal. The car roared back and tore the left front door right off. She stopped the car in the driveway, absolutely panic-stricken. What would Harry say? His brand-new station wagon!

She crept into the house and knelt down beside the couch and prayed to God for forgiveness for this terrible thing she did. Then she prayed to Harry for the same deal, including taking his keys—that was extra. When she finished praying, Harry opened one eye and said, "Whaddahellsamatter with you, crazee sonofabitch."

Another day Grandma Rosie was driving out from town in the old Chevy. She had her young granddaughter with her and was drifting along somewhat faster than the speed limit. Suddenly a patrol car came up behind them with siren howling. Rose pulled over and as she was doing so said to young Christine, grumbling away, "It must be them boys [her grandsons] he is after." Little Christine replied, "No, Grandma, he is after you."

Rosie was a great person and I had a lot of affection for her. There was nothing phony about Rosie, or Harry either for that matter; she was a real Christian who practised her religious beliefs in her daily living.

Harry was somewhat like myself: neither of us could stand a hypocrite. You could be crooked, irreligious, or just plain stupid, but we had no time for bullshit. He always gave me good, practical advice based on solid horse-trader's logic. It is surprising what you can learn from an old horse trader without benefit of university professors or sociologists.

## Don't Shoot from the Saddle

After I had been working in Quesnel awhile and had got to know some of the people in the back country, I made up a bunch of practical first-aid kits with the help of the guys at Spencer-Dickie Drugs. I left them with dependable people in strategic locations away out in the boondocks. These were not the type of kits set up by certain bandage companies that contain 500 yards of bandage but nothing with which you could bandage a sprained ankle, splint a broken leg, or treat an infection. We put up the kits in sturdy plastic lunch buckets, rust proof, everything well labelled, with instructions for use. I left one of these kits with Bunch Trudeau at Euchiniko Lakes, about 150 miles out.

She told me about an RCMP officer who really appreciated some of her 292s for pain when he put a .44 revolver slug through his lower leg while travelling out beyond their place. He was leading a pack horse behind his saddle horse and had his revolver in the holster with all the slots in the cylinder loaded. The lead rope happened to flick the hammer on a loaded cylinder, setting off the .44 bullet. The slug struck him in the lower leg, passing between the two bones and out the opposite side. The shock knocked him off his horse and he came to lying on the ground, with his horse grazing nearby.

He wrapped a bandage of some sort around his leg, hobbled over to his horse, and was able to get on; he then caught his pack horse and headed down the back trail to Trudeaus'. By the time he got back there, two to three hours' ride, I guess his leg pain was getting about all he could handle.

Bunch and Oscar helped him off his horse and got him lying down while Bunch gave him a couple of 292s for the pain. I'll bet he appreciated getting a little pain relief. Bunch cleaned and dressed the wound, gave him some of the antibiotic we put in the kit and more 292s, and kept him off his feet with the leg elevated. He recovered.

I don't think he rode with the hammer on a loaded cylinder after that. Pan Phillips warned me about riding with a bullet in the gun chamber a long time ago, and I have never forgotten. He also told me that most of those old cowboys seldom shot from the saddle. He said it might be OK in Hollywood, but often in real life the horse you were riding was a bronc not too well broke. If there was some bad-tempered animal on the scene you might end up being bucked off and on your back, gazing into the eyes of a very unfriendly grizzly or such.

They brought an American hunter in from out by Tahardy Lake who wasn't as lucky as the man Bunch looked after. This guy had somehow shot himself in the upper leg with a big .44 or .45 six-gun. I think he had been into the booze.

My old friend Jed Campbell and I both liked to hunt, and we were known to party on occasion, but for us, when the guns came out, the liquor was put away. The same went for work. One of Jed's comments was "Any damn fool can get drunk on Saturday night, but it takes a good man to get to work on Monday morning." Jed was always there for work on Monday.

Anyway, this American's friends got him on a wagon and brought him on the long trip, about a day I think, and loaded him in a pickup truck for the remainder of the trip to hospital in Quesnel. When I went into the examining room to see him, I was hit with the unmistakable stink of gas gangrene. It is said that if you have ever smelled gas gangrene, you never forget it, and I *had* smelled gas gangrene. We took him to the OR where we did a high midthigh amputation of his left leg. We filled him full of several million units of crystalline penicillin, gave him gas gangrene antiserum, and he lived to tell the tale.

## Prescription: Trauma

Quite often cases that looked like real catastrophes turned out not too bad. Ninety percent of emergencies seemed to happen at night, most often the middle of the night. Accidents in the bush always had a higher incidence in the few days before freeze-up and break-up, indicating very strongly that it doesn't pay to rush and take chances while in hazardous situations. The absolute idiocy of alcohol in the workplace should scarcely need mention.

This particular night they brought an unconscious teenager in from upper Baker Creek. He had been kicked in the head by a horse: the middle of his forehead was pushed in to a depth of three-quarters of an inch in the distinct outline of a horseshoe. One of my co-workers intubated him, ran some oxygen, and hyperventilated him so we could turn down a skin flap and elevate the depressed bone to examine what was under it. The dura (membrane) lining the skull was lacerated. This meant that the barrier that usually kept bacteria from spreading up to the front of the brain from the nasal cavity was torn. The frontal lobes of the brain were contused (bruised), with some lacerated areas.

We trimmed out some of the lacerated brain substance and cauterized the bleeding points with the electro-cautery. We filled the whole area with antibiotic. Next we prepared an area on his right thigh and made a long incision in order to take out a square of fascia (tissue) big enough to make a large patch to lay over the lacerated dura. We sutured the patch into place, put the skull bone back where it belonged, and repaired the skin. After the bone pressing on his brain was pried out, the teenager regained consciousness and in a few days was on the road to recovery.

Sometimes an accident even improved the worker. A man was brought into the ER after a log fell off a load and struck him on the head, tearing his ear half off. We sewed his ear back on and it took okay. His skull X-ray showed a fracture all right, but it was not depressed. He was unconscious initially, but regained consciousness in the Intensive Care Unit and eventually recovered and was ready to go back to work. The Workers' Compensation Board wrote me to ask for a report on any long-term mental deficit or personality changes. I was hard put to come up with a report for them. Old Bill was not university material at the best of times, but he was supposed to be a good well-witcher and had located water for many local well-drillers. I was able to report to the WCB that he was a better well-witcher after the log hit him on the head than he had been before.

## Lay off the Love

One young fellow fell in through the emergency room door one night and the nurses fortunately found him; he was having serious breathing trouble. He told them that after a fight with his girlfriend he took his gun in the car and drove five miles up the road, where he got out and shot himself. He must not have been any better a shot than he was a lover, as he missed his heart, putting a bullet through his left lung instead, and giving himself a tension pneumothorax. We got him in a treatment room, stuck in a chest tube under local anaesthetic, and relieved the pressure build-up so that he could breathe. He was able to get his tube out and go home in a few days. I told him I thought he had shot the wrong person, but if he persisted in trying to shoot himself he should use a shorter barrelled gun and aim it at his head.

Sometimes emergencies weren't quite what they were cracked up to be. One night I got called in to see a man in the ER. The nurse said that he told her at the desk that he had fallen on a bar and injured his pelvis. She asked him if it would be a Workers' Compensation case and he said he guessed so. When I got there she had the WCB papers partly made out—name, date of birth, and so on.

When we got him in the examining room, away from the crowd in the waiting room, we got a different case history. This guy just didn't look like a pelvic injury to me. I picked up the WCB form, and after studying it for a minute I asked him, "Did you say you fell *on* a bar or *in* a bar?" He squirmed a little and didn't answer. I then asked him, "Would there have been a woman on this bar when you fell on it?" He grinned sheepishly and admitted that he guessed there was. I proceeded to crumple up the WCB report and told him I really didn't think we should send it in.

I then proceeded to examine the parts that needed examining and confirmed that he had a full-blown case of gonorrhoea. The nurse went

141

to get the 10 million units of penicillin, and instead of submitting a WCB report I told him that before we could treat him we had to fill a VD contact report for Public Health. Things started to get a little humorous for me, if not for him. I asked him if he knew this woman from whom he had picked up his dose of gonorrhoea. He said, "I should, I'm supposed to marry her in two weeks." I suggested to him that they wait at least until they were both cleared up.

Sure enough, in the *Quesnel Observer* two weeks later there was a full-scale wedding write-up, complete with snow-white wedding dress. Some people have no class!

Not long after this we had an unusual hunting accident in the ER on a Saturday afternoon. The same red-headed ER nurse was on duty. She asked me if I would see this man who had come in from a hunting trip. She had a tongue-in-cheek attitude for this one.

He was a well-known businessman from New Westminster who had been hunting out in the Nazko area. He got his moose the first day, so he had been whiling away the time at the camp of his faithful guide, specifically with this faithful guide's promiscuous daughter. By the time he got to Quesnel he knew he was in trouble.

This was in the early days of prepaid medicine, when the patient received in the mail an itemized account for treatment. The gent was most anxious to stay off our hospital books and said he would prefer to pay cash for any treatment. I told him that, as a courtesy from one outdoorsman to another, there would be no charge from me for medical treatment.

We gave him the usual 10 million units of penicillin and notified Public Health of the contact. We further suggested to him that he go hunt chukars for a week at Wallachin before going home to his wife. He went away quite happy. As he was driving away with his friends, the ER nurse noticed that we didn't have a diagnosis entered in the book for him.

She said, "We have to put down *something*."

"Just enter it as 'hunting accident,'" I told her. I expected some kind of backlash from Victoria, but we never did hear another word on that case.

Another incident that occurred might seem funny when it happens to someone else but not to you. A fellow came up from the coast to stay awhile on his brother's farm because his nerves were bad and he wanted to relax. He was working with a farm tractor, running a machine off the power take-off, when he got too close to the high-speed shaft; it caught his pants and ripped off the crotch as well as the skin off his scrotum, leaving both testicles hanging in the breeze. The testicles themselves were intact, as was their blood supply. When we got him to the operating room and asleep, we simply made a pocket in the skin of his inner thighs and tucked in the testicles, one on each side. He would never be a jockey, and he would just have to travel on foot.

The next afternoon his brother phoned in from the farm and in his slow drawl said, "Say Doc, I guess it wouldn't be any good to you now, but we found the skin off his balls on top of the diesel fuel tank." I told him thanks but that we made out OK and his brother was doing all right, especially since we put him on some tranquillizers. Unfortunately the poor guy committed suicide a few weeks later. I guess we were remiss in not sending him for intensive psychotherapy. We thought that since he had a pair of testicles in good working order, that should be enough.

# TWELVE

# Bears in the Backyard

## Don't Shoot a Bear in the Brisket

A case that could have been disastrous involved my old friend and big-game guide Frank Cushman, who got chased into the lake by a grizzly at his hunting camp.

It was late October and the last of his hunters had left. His son, Tim, had gone up Littlefield Creek to fix a trapline cabin, and Frank was going to trail his pack horses out the next day. He decided that since some pack horses would be "empty," he should take a tour around and look for a moose for winter meat.

He picked up his .300 Weatherby Magnum and a handful of shells and was walking along the fringe of timber not far from the cabin. As he was passing another old cabin they used for a storehouse, he noticed that the plastic on the window was torn. At that instant he heard a movement in the brush beside him and swung his gun around in time to meet a big grizzly charging out at him.

He aimed for the big bear's brisket and fired, but the bear never slowed down. Frank levered in another shell and fired again. He tried to run backwards to get into the clear on the narrow stretch of beach. Next thing he knew he fell backwards into a foot of water and the bear was right in after him.

He lay on his back in the water with his gun across his chest, keeping quite still. The bear stood up on its hind legs beside him and bellowed and slashed the air with its claws. Frank never made a move.

When Frank told me the story, I asked him what he was thinking of just then. He said, "I was wondering where he was going to take the first bite."

After the bear roared and clawed the air for a couple of minutes, he dropped down on all fours, ran around to the other side of Frank, and roared some more. Then he lay down in the water with his back to Frank. He didn't move much, so Frank quietly raised his gun, pointed it at the middle of the bear's backbone, and pulled the trigger. There was a loud "click" that Frank thought could be heard all over the lake. Now the bear would get him for sure.

But nothing happened. Frank carefully raised up on one elbow and looked. The bear's head was in the water and there were circles of bloody froth coming from its nose.

Still watching the bear closely, he quietly got to his feet, waded to shore, and then ran like hell for the cabin. Once inside he changed into dry clothes, picked up a half bottle of Captain Morgan rum sitting on the table, and downed it, straight.

A couple days later, when Frank came to town, he brought in the heart he had removed from the bear. I examined it. The high-velocity bullet had gone in through the bear's brisket and through the heart—which had literally been blown to bits.

With all that damage from Frank's first shot, that old bear had charged out of the brush and across a strip of beach into the water, where it stood up. The bear then waved its arms and roared for one or two minutes before it ran around to the other side of Frank and roared some more—all after its heart was completely shattered. That was a scary encounter and we were glad it was the bear we did the post mortem on and not Frank. Blowing a bear's heart to pieces is obviously not a good way of stopping him.

## Don't Mess With Mama

Frank's son Tim was another guy I must list among Cariboo characters, though he was quite a bit younger than most of us who were cavorting around in earlier days. In fact, he stayed with my wife and me when he was going to high school in Quesnel. Later we were out on quite a few interesting escapades in the hills. Nothing, but nothing, ever got Tim excited or flustered, and he had a quiet sense of humour.

One day Tim was taking some inexperienced dudes out on a trail ride. One of these guys reminded Tim that some of them hadn't ridden very much. Tim told him not to let that worry them; some of the horses hadn't been ridden very much either.

Another day Tim, my ten-year-old daughter Marissa (Mouse), and I were taking a string of pack horses down from the mountains. We were on a steep, narrow trail down a timbered sidehill. Tim had four dogs with him, all half-malamute and half-airedale. He said he wanted to see if they were any good.

We were halfway down the side hill when I heard this great roar and snarling and growling ahead. Tim had a grizzly cub up a tree above him, and the old sow was trying her best to get at him. Tim was off his horse, which had scrambled up the bank out of the way, and the four dogs were all over this old bear just a-snapping and dodging. They practically dragged her back down the trail. Tim was balanced on a windfall ten feet off the ground, trying to get some rifle shells out of a sock in which he had tied them. In his usual calm voice he said, "Say Al, do you think you can get them pack horses turned around?"

So I got "them pack horses" turned around pretty smartly and pointed up the back-trail. Mouse and I took them back about 300 yards and held them there. In the meantime I had my own gun out of the holster. Tim said those dogs put that old grizzly right out of there and didn't even get a scratch on one of them, so we decided they were pretty good bear dogs. He didn't want to shoot the bear because she had a cub with her. We called the dogs back and kept them with us for a half-hour while the old sow came and got her cub down out of the tree and took off. We then continued on our way.

When we were in Frank's hunting camp at Krugar Lake, the four paying customers, who came for caribou and moose, slept in the cabin, while Frank and Tim and I slept in a tent by the lakeshore. A big chunk of the front of the tent was ripped open and we could see out. When it got to be five o'clock in the morning, and daylight, we could look out and see the morning procession of grizzly bears along the beach. We didn't bother them and they didn't bother us. Instead they steadfastly ignored us as they strolled silently past on their way to and from the area where the caribou meat was cut and trimmed for wrapping and flying out.

The same thing went for grizzly and pack horses. They all ranged in the same swamps, the horses eating slough grass in the open spots and the bears eating plants and roots and anything else to their liking. I do not know of one horse that was killed or injured by a bear. The guides and outfitters tried to avoid situations where we had to shoot a bear. For one thing, we were conservationists and didn't kill what we didn't need, and secondly, grizzly were part of the outfitter's cash crop. He saved them for paying clients.

## "Stealing" a Bear's Private Stock

Tom Moffat and I made a couple of interesting trips into the Prophet River country. On this one trip, when Frank Cushman was with us, we had bear trouble. Everything went fine on our way up. We visited with our friends at Trutch Mountain while we rounded up pack horses, we crossed the Prophet River at the good crossing, and everything was peachy. About two days in from the river crossing we unpacked on an old burned-off willow flat near a big beaver dam and made camp for the night just off the pack trail.

After supper, while we were having coffee, we heard the sound of a bear bawling. It seemed to be about a quarter of a mile downriver from us. The cries were repeated, this time a little closer. It quieted down, the horses finished grazing and were tied up in a clump of jack pines close by, and we rolled up in our bedrolls, with our rifles beside us. Tom and I bedded down in a three-man nylon tent and Frank threw a tarp over a leaning spruce tree close by. He said he would rather put up with a bear prowling around than listen to us guys snore.

At about one o'clock in the morning I woke up. Tom was poking me in the ribs and whispering, "That sonofabitch is just outside the tent." Next I heard Snap. Snap. Crunch—the sound of the bear walking right by the tent.

I said to Tom, "If that bear comes in through the side of the tent I don't want to be caught bare-assed and bare-footed." We quickly put our pants and boots on.

Moffat whispered, "I wonder if Frank heard him." At that moment we heard a zziiii-p as Frank unzipped his sleeping bag. With our guns in hand we walked over in the dark to the remains of our campfire. I stoked it up and with my rifle in one hand and the dishpan in the other I fanned it into a decent flame. We had two flashlights but we didn't want to chance the batteries wearing out at this particular time. Now we could hear the twigs breaking as he walked back and forth in the brush just beyond the firelight and beyond where we could get a flashlight on him. We waited a few minutes for him to make his move.

We weren't too worried as we were out in the open, we all had good guns, and we knew how to use them, but we wanted to get back to sleep if that damned bear would settle down or, better still, just take off. We did not want to shoot in his direction and wound him, but we would like to scare him off. We decided that if we shot just over him he would either run or charge us. So while two of us kept our rifles ready, the other one let a volley go over the bear's head. He gave a snort and crashed off through the underbrush. We went back to bed with our rifles beside us and heard him bawl a couple more times in the early morning, but at some distance away across the beaver dam. We slept soundly—our snoring was probably enough to keep him at a respectable distance. Through all this performance our horses remained quiet where they were tied up with their bells on, quite close to our camp.

Next morning we had breakfast and were collecting our horses, ready to pack up, when we stumbled onto the remains of a moose kill only 20 yards behind our tent. No wonder the bear was indignant—we had camped

*A rough comparison—our hand vs. a bear track—hopefully not the bear that walked by our tent while camping with Tom Moffat and Frank Cushman.*

practically on top of his dinner table. If he had come back we would have apologized to him for lousing up his supper. We packed and saddled up and headed out. We heard no more of that bear, but saw his big grizzly claw tracks a few yards up the trail.

When we were getting back towards the Minnaker River and our vehicle late one afternoon, we saw a humorous sight by an open area in the muskeg. No less than six pickup trucks of various kinds, obviously hunting rigs, all lined up in a bunch, and there on the edge of the opening was a big bull moose gazing at the line-up with a contemplative look. It was difficult to get the setting sun, the moose, and the vehicles all lined up without getting our horses into the muskeg, so we did not get a picture. We should have.

We usually had some bears around at home as well as at campsites. Our place at Dragon Lake had a creek running through the lower side of our yard, and this was a favourite fishing hole for bears—usually black bears. They generally left us alone, and as long as they kept their distance, we didn't bother them. Our sled dogs barked only if the bears came up in the yard.

One night when we came home the dogs were making a hell of a racket. It was a foggy, drizzly night and I thought there must be something in the yard, so I grabbed my automatic twelve-gauge and a flashlight and went out back to see what was there. The first thing I saw was this big old black bear coming right at me. Fred Wagner was staying with us and he was yelling at me, "Shoot the booger, shoot the booger, he's coming at you."

I waited until he was 30 or 40 feet from me and then I drove him with the shotgun. It knocked him down. When he got up he turned and ran for the thick brush by the creek. I gave him another blast while he was on the run. In the morning we found him lying dead in the brush. He had charged me because my wife had left some suet low down in a tree for the birds and he thought that was his private stock.

On another occasion I heard a great commotion in the chicken yard. I grabbed my little Browning .308 and ran up, thinking it must be coyotes or neighbourhood dogs. The hens were all crowded into one corner of the pen but there were no dogs or coyotes to see. As I was looking around for the culprits I suddenly felt the hair rise on the back of my neck. I looked up and there in a poplar tree, about 20 feet above me, was a young bear. About ten feet above him was another one. I shot the first one and he tumbled down; then I shot the other one, but he got fouled up in a fork of the tree and I had to get the power saw and fall the tree away from the fence. That was the first time I ever had bears after my chickens, but they tell me it does happen.

Grizzlies don't have to be away out in the wilderness either. Years later I shot one in our back yard. On that occasion I had been away from home working at Barkerville for a week, and when I got home my second wife Judi, whom I married in 1979, told me that she hadn't had any sleep for the last three nights because the dogs had been raising such a racket. They didn't usually make that much fuss for black bears. I was telling Judi how to tell a grizzly from ordinary bears—they have a bigger, wider head, wide snout, longer claws, and a very pronounced hump at the shoulders. I told her they could be any colour, including solid black like a black bear, and I also told her that anytime she saw a bear with that big hump over the shoulders she should get the

*My gun barrel points to the height a big grizzly smeared mud on a spruce tree we found on a trip to the McGregor Mountains in 1977.*

hell out of there whether she was on horseback or on foot, and she should not run but slowly back up, keeping the bear in view.

Later that day, just outside our house, she saw a big brown silver-tip bear standing up on its hind feet; when it dropped down on all fours she was pretty sure it was a grizzly. Judi quickly got in the house and grabbed a gun and some shells. At that point she looked out the back door and saw me coming down from the field. Our two small housedogs had chased the bear out of sight. When she told me what had happened I looked at the gun she had brought down and knew it was a little light for bear. I got my Model 70 Winchester .338 Magnum and headed down to where the bear had been.

In the meantime our neighbour, Ron Wiwchar, came over with his 30:06; Judi had called him before I arrived back. The two of us carefully walked down towards the creek where the bear was last seen. I thought it was funny the bear didn't "tree" the way they usually do with the dogs after them. When we got down to the creek I said to Ron, "Let's take a look in the mud

*A bear skin keeps me warm Cariboo-style at a cabin in the McGregor Mountains.*

and see what kind of tracks he's making." We were just standing watching and listening for a minute. Then I saw this pair of ears coming through the underbrush. That bear was creeping along quiet as a cat. All I could see was his head, eyes, and ears. I thought he was pretty wide between the ears for a black bear, so I quietly brought up my rifle and let him have it right between the eyes. He dropped and never even twitched. We stepped it off and it was 90 feet to where the bear was. He was three or four years old. It is said that grizzly that age will stalk humans for food if they are hungry, and he was sure stalking us. I don't know whether he thought my wife, Ron, or I would have made the best evening meal.

Another evening I had a black bear up a tree and I wanted to show it to Judi, who was coming out from town in a short while. So when the bear started climbing down the tree I scared her back up again. I had a big branch off a tree and I banged it against the trunk of the cottonwood she was in and she climbed back up.

About that time, somebody started practising take-off and landing with their float plane on the lake just north of our house. On every takeoff they flew directly over the bear—and the bear got a little more upset with each pass. She was snapping her teeth and fidgeting around on the big branch she was sitting on, reaching out and biting off all the smaller branches. The plane took another pass and she got really upset. She started down the tree and I banged on the cottonwood with my wooden club and yelled at her to get back up. I was wishing Judi would get out here. On the third pass of the aircraft, right overhead, it got too much for the bear. Suddenly she just let go of everything she had in her urinary bladder. I didn't get any on me, but a few feet away I heard this big swish and a plop as the water hit the ground. Judi arrived a couple of minutes later. I showed her the bear in the tree and told her she just missed seeing that float plane scare the piss out of that bear.

## THIRTEEN

# Mosquito Tea and the Anahim Stampede

### Mosquito Tea

For years I never missed an Anahim Stampede. I was house physician and used to look after most of their accident victims. At the very least you were guaranteed to see a lot of local colour as well as meeting lots of old-time friends: guys like Lester Dorsey, Pan Phillips, Roy Mulvahill, Randolph Mulvahill, Dwayne Witte from Teepee Heart Ranch, Alex and Ann Paxton from Alexis Creek, and Woody Woodward.

The only time I ever saw Lester afraid was one night at the Anahim Stampede when we let the tent down on Pan Phillips and his wife, Betty. When he heard Betty start to swear, Lester left me behind like I was standing still.

That was the same night, I believe, when Lester, Gertrude Fraser, Larry Smith, and I decided to put a horse in the dance hall at the stampede, just for the hell of it. In the morning there was a helluva commotion when this girl found her barrel horse missing from her camp. We were all very quiet on the subject. Soon somebody opened the dance hall door and there, standing among piles of horse manure, was the lost horse. Once the horse was found, the girl did not pursue the issue—it was just something you might expect at the Anahim Stampede.

The pack trip over and back was always an interesting experience. One time we were riding back as far as the Home Ranch with Pan and Betty, Ed Adams, and some others when we stopped in Corkscrew Basin for the night. Pan's routine was to pull up in a sheltered spot, tie the horses, and grab an axe right away to cut some dry wood. We had a great fire going with dry spruce and pine, and Betty got a big wide-mouthed pot on the fire to make tea. Clouds of mosquitoes flew over us, and when they hit the flames they fell into the pot. The tea was turning into stew.

Pan growled, "Betty, get those damned mosquitoes out of the tea— I don't mind them in the stew but I can't stand them in the tea."

## One Mean Horse

In the summer of 1985 Geoff Thomas, Tom Moffat, and I trailered our horses out to the 164-kilometre marker on Michel Creek. We rode in on a seismic line to the Itcha Mountains, then on over the Itchas to Anahim. We camped overnight at Michel Creek Road. After our trip, Thomas told the Williams Lake Tribune that our personal hygiene consisted of "standing in the creek until your feet got numb, throwing water over yourself until your body got numb, and then running like hell to the camp, hoping the mosquitoes didn't carry you away."

We had two broke saddle horses, two half-broke colts, and one crazy gelding that I had given to Geoff Thomas. I had ridden this gelding mostly down on the mud flats at the end of the lake at our place, and he was broke to neck rein, back up, change leads, and all that, but always had to have his little buck when you started out in the morning.

When he was a yearling he was a good young colt, and sensible. Then I sold him as a stallion to some guys with a string of pack and saddle horses, and he was abused. One of these guys got a Clyde stallion that he wanted to use, so this poor little horse got roped and castrated and roughed up quite a bit. I didn't get paid for him, so we agreed that I would take him back.

He was running with a bunch out in the meadows 150 miles northeast of Quesnel, so I jumped my saddle horse in the trailer and went out and got him. One of the boys told me where the bunch was ranging, so I rounded them up and chased the whole bunch into a corral at the ranch, where we lassoed him. I got a halter on him and loaded him, along with my saddle horse, into the trailer and hauled them back home to Dragon Lake.

By this time the horse had lost all faith in humans and didn't trust anybody. Every time I got on him he had to have his little buck. By now I'm getting a few years on me and it *hurts* when I hit the ground. I never did fancy myself as a bronc buster, and since Geoff got along with this horse better than I did, I just gave him the horse.

I think Geoff looked on it as a challenge, and on the trip over the Itchas to Anahim he got challenged every morning, even though we put in a tough day the day before. Some days he even had a little buck when we were coming into camp for the night. This didn't bother Geoff; both he and the horse enjoyed the go-round.

*Geoff Thomas leads our horses on the Snowshoe Plateau.*

One day we switched things around: Tom rode my good saddle mare; I rode his young mare, who was going pretty well; Geoff rode Tom's horse; and we packed the crazy young grey and another one. I was leading this grey and everything was going fine as we went along the trail across this big jack-pine flat. I was having a fine time on Tom's mare, but this little grey airhead decided it was too peaceful for his liking.

He started to hump up as we were going along and started to crowd my young horse and bump her on the rump with the corner of the pack box. She didn't like that much, so she started to get that funny look in her eye. Every time he would boost her on the ass with the pack box, she would crow hop a little more and I could see that she was about ready to cut loose with the next jump. I didn't want to find myself riding a bucking mare through the jack pines with this other goofball trying to run over us, banging my knees with the pack box, so I just pulled a flying switch on him.

I threw the lead rope over his neck and pulled my horse in a quick move out of his way and let him go by. The next few minutes were very interesting. That little horse ducked his head between his front legs and he sunfished and spiralled and bucked like a Brahma bull. But he really didn't want to leave us out in that strange country far from home, so he just bucked in a circle around us.

Eventually he got the top pack off and then proceeded to scatter the contents of the boxes. Tom's camera flew out and landed on the moss, then a series of other gear, then my bottle of O.P. rum landed on another clump of moss. I was thinking, "The Lord helps amateur packers as well as working girls."

He eventually got bucked out and headed for Tom, who was sitting on his horse watching the show. I got off my horse and quietly walked over and got his lead rope. The packsaddle had spun around and one pack box was underneath him. As soon as I touched his lead rope he went into orbit again and tried to jump over Tom and his horse. Tom quickly slid off the opposite side of his horse. We reached under and undid both cinches on the gelding. We tied the goofy bugger to a tree with a sturdy rope and circled around, picking up the scattered gear while he settled his nerves.

We then replaced the packsaddle, cinched her down good and tight, and repacked all the stuff recovered from among the jack pines. We led that goofball gelding from a quiet horse for the rest of the day without further mishap.

## A Herd of Caribou and a Blonde

When we got out of the jack pines we crossed a swale towards a ridge to the left of a flat-topped mountain. We then descended a steep and brushy sidehill into what we later found out was Smoke Valley. We crossed the valley floor, then climbed up an equally steep and brushy mountainside to get back out of the valley. This got us up on a long treeless ridge running south toward where three valleys came together. We didn't want to get any farther west, because I had crossed there with Pan Phillips via Corkscrew Creek several years ago and I knew there was thick timber that way, hard to take pack horses through. So we turned south on the ridge with the thought that one of the three valleys would lead us toward Anahim. We rode the length of the ridge and started down into the valley.

Next thing we knew, a herd of 45 caribou came galloping out to meet us. I had my .308 on my saddle and was just thinking how tasty a steak off one of those young bulls would be, although it was out of season of course, when we were greeted by this attractive blonde with short shorts, hiking boots, and a can of insect spray.

She came bounding out on the slope below us and I thought Moffat and Geoff were going to break their horses' legs getting down there. She told us she was a graduate student from the University of Victoria, doing a study on the caribou herd. She showed us where she was camped across the valley. We asked her about trails or blazes in the three valleys ahead, but she didn't know very much about that. She thought there were some blazes on the trees going out of the valley at the lower end. After we left her we met another larger herd of caribou, about 80, similar to the first herd, tame and dumb. I thought it would not be a good idea to shoot one of this girl's pet caribou, so we didn't.

When we got to where the valleys came together we took the bottom one and, sure enough, came to an old trail with blazes. A little farther on, another trail joined this one and there were shod saddle horse tracks on it going south. From the look of the tracks we could see that these horses were moving right along and we bet those cowboys were heading for one place, and that would be the beer garden at the Anahim Stampede. Then our own pace quickened a little. We carried on to where the trail joined the well-used Corkscrew Basin trail, with more shod horse tracks going out. We crossed Corkscrew Creek and came to a high rail fence with a locked gate and a sign that said "No Trespassing."

I thought, "What an A-hole to block off a well-travelled main trail." We went around his big pasture, which took us an extra half-hour to travel, but we did get through a broken-down gate and on our way. We found out later that the man who blocked the trail was an American smartass who was not too popular.

We moved right along until we found some abandoned buildings at Pete Vogelaar's old ranch, half a day's ride to Anahim, and we camped there. The ranch had a good creek and a big corral with lots of grass. There was an old shed with lots of pack rats, too, but the roof didn't leak.

The next day we rode past the bucking chutes at Anahim in midafternoon to the loud cheers of the crowd; the announcer on the P.A. system told them that Doc Holley and Tom Moffat and Doctor Geoff Thomas had just arrived from Quesnel via Upper Blackwater River and over the Itcha Mountains. We enjoyed the whoop-up, and when it was over we headed back with nice weather.

While at the stampede we met up with Bill Lehman, who told us about a trail he used to take hunters up to his guide area in the Itchas. We followed this trail, which shortened the travel time quite a bit—an example of the helpful bits of info you can pick up sitting around a campfire but would never see in a provincial parks guide book. Those books are like government campsites—they have great outhouses, but are always short of firewood.

# FOURTEEN

# Frontier Women

I would be remiss if I didn't mention some of our women guide outfitters in this book. I'm sure there will be a few that I miss, but I will mention some.

Bunch Trudeau at Euchiniko Lakes was a colourful frontier woman. She and Oscar guided moose and bear hunters and had a small ranch. One time three grizzly bears wandered into their yard while Bunch was washing clothes. She left the clothes for a minute, got her rifle and shot the bears, then finished her laundry; the hides are now rugs on the floor.

Betty Franks was a statuesque, attractive, originally honey blonde woman who trapped and guided up the North Arm of Quesnel Lake. Betty was a pretty good musher and had some good dogs, huskies crossed with Japanese bear dogs. She and I also raised some sled dogs from her Siberian huskies bred to my big Irish wolfhound. Those dogs weren't as good as we hoped for, however. (The strongest, toughest dog I ever owned was a cross between a malamute and an Eskimo sled dog. We called him Mukluk. It seemed to suit him.)

Evelyn Knauf was another Cariboo guide. She made the headlines of the *Cariboo Observer* by hitting a local cop on Front Street and knocking him six feet straight back by measurement. Evelyn and her husband were good friends of mine.

Another Cariboo woman, June Olson, though not a big-game guide, was a patient and an old friend of mine. I knew the story of how June had beat this black bear over the head with a two-by-four to get it out of her pigpen.

She also told me about the time that some thugs thought they could force her to fill their tank up, as well as her own, at a deserted key-lock station. She said this one guy told her that she was going to fill their tank up. She said she was *not*. When he tried to lay a hand on her, she kicked him right in the nuts and he rolled over in the snow, clutching his crotch. She turned to the next guy and said, "Do you want to be next?" He quickly backed off. At that opportune moment a cop car saw the commotion and drove up, loaded the thugs in the bun wagon, and hauled them off to the jug. June told me, "Those cops said I only done one thing wrong and that was that I didn't kick him hard enough."

## Hauling Betty to Barkerville

Elizabeth (Betty) Wendle was in her late 80s when she died in Quesnel. She and her late husband, Joe, were old-timers in the Barkerville area. Joe was a prospector and promoter. I remember looking after them in the 1950s when they used to come to Quesnel to winter at the Cascade Auto Court to get away from the long cold winters in Barkerville. Old Elizabeth was a real Annie Oakley and had three grizzly bear hides hanging on a wall in Barkerville to prove it. Betty Wendle Creek, on the north side of Isaac Lake, was named after her. She was a nice old girl, and Alex and Gertrude Fraser looked after her pretty well after old Joe died.

Anyway, in the middle of the winter, Betty Wendle a-turned up her toes and a funeral service was held. Afterwards she was to be taken to Barkerville to be buried in the Barkerville Cemetery, with a short graveside service. Alex Fraser and I each offered to take a load of old-timers up with us.

I got a bad start on the day when I had to change a flat tire just after I got my car started out of the yard, so I was late for the funeral service. I had good studded tires on my old Chrysler, so when the young undertaker's assistant told us he didn't think the hearse would make it, I offered to tow him. Alex also had a good car, so we thought that between the two of us we could get him there.

I couldn't help thinking to myself that I had entered the town of Wells under all sorts of conditions, but this would be the first time I arrived towing a hearse. We all made it. Before we left the funeral chapel, however, we received a phone call that instructed us to go to the house of Herb Hadfield, the postmaster, to wait until the grave-digging detail was completed.

This was in midwinter and the ground was frozen harder than a crowbar handle. Apparently a grave-digging crew had been sent out on three successive days under the leadership of Kingsley Foreman, but each time they never got past the Jack of Clubs bar. Now, on the final day, they still had seven or eight inches of frozen ground to get out before the casket would be covered. King wanted to use powder, but several old-timers said absolutely "No!" Old Bill Hong and others guessed that if they turned King Foreman loose with a box of dynamite, they would be picking up pieces of Old Joe, who occupied the other half of the double plot, from all over the sidehill.

Meanwhile we detoured through to Hadfield's to fill in some time. Herb and Betty had a pretty good bar set up. After getting our coats off I looked around, and it was immediately plain to me that a round of good stiff drinks was in order for the whole crowd.

Nell Dowsett and Johnny Leonard, who were in my car, grabbed their whisky glasses like they feared they'd never see another one. I introduced the two young fellows who had been dispatched from Quesnel to do the official honours, and one look at them told me that they *really* needed a good drink. They were both shivering like a cat in a snowdrift and could barely hold a glass. After a good shot for each of them, poured by whoever was tending bar, I could see the circulation slowly returning. The young preacher could barely form words when he first arrived and now he was quite coherent. The young funeral director, who was filling in for his boss, had a terrible tremor to start with, but after they had a second shot of good whisky they both became quite jocular.

We could see that they would not only survive this day, but they might even begin to enjoy it. The rest of the assorted guests were appreciating Hadfield's whisky, and it had the makings of a good lively party. Nell Dowsett regaled us with stories of Joe Wendle's claim-jumping activities, and various others added their bit. We finally got word that the crew was down to grade level and we didn't want to keep Old Betty waiting.

The gravesite was steep and slippery, and some of the designated pallbearers were too tipsy to negotiate the path. Alex and I both had good winter snowboots with cleats on the soles, so we were elected pinch-hitters for some of the pallbearers. We were able to hold back the others on the downhill grade and successfully swing the casket into position. The young preacher by now was in good form and gave a powerful and eloquent send-off. The young funeral director helped some of the more tipsy mourners to stay on their feet. After the service was completed we got our passengers into the cars and headed back to Quesnel. As funeral services go, everybody seemed to think that it went quite well and a good time was had by all.

## Message Time

One day in the middle of the long Cariboo winter, Sergeant Stinson decided to take me and my medical bag on a tour of the boondocks out west to check on isolated settlers. The Quesnel detachment arranged for the RCMP Beaver aircraft on skis to come in and pick us up. Stinson, a constable, and I would visit Batnunni Smith at Batnunni Lake to the northwest; Oscar and Bunch Trudeau, 150 miles west on Euchiniko Lake;

and Pan Phillips at the Home Ranch, about 200 miles west of Quesnel. Most of these people had not seen anybody all winter. We decided that on this trip we would check first on Oscar and Bunch Trudeau, so Stinson sent them a message on the CKCQ radio show "Message Time," letting them know that we hoped to get out that way.

We took off and headed west on a clear winter day. When we got out to the Blackwater River we flew along the valley and saw large numbers of moose basking in the winter sun on the south-facing slopes. There was nothing to disturb them and the scene was a picture of tranquillity. We eventually came to Euchiniko, which is really just a wide spot in the Blackwater River.

As Harry Haycock, the pilot, made a large swing to come into the bay in front of the Trudeaus' cabin, he remarked that he would sure like to know how much ice we had on the lake. As we straightened out to come in for a landing, we saw tramped in the snow in big letters "12 INCHES ICE." The Trudeaus expected us and had figured that the pilot might just want to know this information. I knew from experience in the north that to land a Beaver, the pilot needs seven inches of clear ice-- for a Norseman, a little more.

We landed, taxied up to the shore, and hiked up to the cabin. Bunch met us at the door. As we were getting our coats off she was bustling around getting coffee. She apologized because she couldn't stop shaking. Then she told us what happened.

Bunch and Oscar were moving their small herd of cattle to another meadow when this big Hereford bull suddenly turned, charged her, and knocked her off her horse and down in the snow. He had her between his horns and was rolling her back and forth in the two feet of snow on the ground. Oscar was close by so he pulled out this 9 mm Luger from his holster and creased the bull in the neck, knocking it off Bunch. She scrambled up, caught her horse, and climbed back on. She said she was not hurt except that her ribs were sore. Oscar was taking the cows the rest of the way to the meadow and would be in shortly. She said she felt silly.

Stinson and I looked at each other and made no comment. They hadn't seen another human since last November, and if she had suffered severe chest injuries she would have been out of luck, yet here we were with an aircraft and a doctor—how fortuitous.

In a few minutes Oscar arrived, tied up his horse, and came in to visit. He poured himself a hot cup of coffee, stretched out his legs, and told us, "Came near to having a little accident out there this morning."

Nobody said anything else for a minute or two and I was waiting for the punchline.

Bunch asked, "How's the bull, Oscar?"

# FIFTEEN

# Fake Cowboys and Real Cowboys

## Driving Team in Barkerville

During the summer of 1987 I had been going pretty steadily in the operating room, with a lot of night work, and both the OR nurses and I were pooped out. So I booked ten days off. On the second day off, my old friend Frank Cushman came along and asked me if I would drive stagecoach for him in Barkerville for a few days. He had fired one of his drivers and he needed someone to fill in.

That was the beginning of a long association with Frank and the teamster business in Barkerville. Frank had a contract with the Parks Branch to supply horses and some wagons and drivers. The Parks Branch owned an old Concorde Stage Coach that Frank drove. He had a regular run up to the top end of town and charged the tourists two to three bucks a ride. He also had a big team of Belgians, Charley and Pride, that he used on a freight wagon to deliver stuff to the various businesses in town since no motor vehicles were allowed inside the front gate.

I drove both stagecoach and freight wagon. The worst nuisance driving stagecoach was change. I swear that when tourists headed out for Barkerville they filled their pockets with $20 bills and nothing else. Frank and I had lots of little jokes going that the rest of them didn't know about and we liked to keep it that way.

All of us working on the streets were supposed to portray life as it was in the 1800s, and we all had street names to go with it. Frank was known as Ned Stout, for whom Stout's Gulch in Barkerville was named. According to early accounts, Ned had collected three arrows in his carcass during an Indian attack in the Fraser Canyon, but had survived to make his way to Barkerville and the gold fields. I took the name of Snodgrass,

*Frank Cushman (top right) and I (bottom left) tore up the Barkerville streets during our stint as street performers for the Parks Branch. Here we are driving Charley and Pride down Main Street (centre).*

a character made famous by a professor of pharmacy at the University of Alberta, Dr. Huston, in his book *The Great Canadian Lover.* Professor Huston had grown up in Ashcroft and at an early age had been imbued with the historical past of Ashcroft, Barkerville, and the Cariboo Road.

In this very humorous book, Snodgrass was portrayed as a teamster who drove one of the slow-moving freight wagons that plodded their way between Ashcroft and Barkerville. Snodgrass was a great teamster and it was said that with his long rawhide whip he could take the testicles off a mosquito on the lead horse's ear without either the mosquito or the horse knowing what happened. Snodgrass had other proficiencies also: he was a great lover. He had a great string of paramours, and at various places along the way Snodgrass would hand over the lines of the slow-moving wagon team to his assistant, have a tryst with some receptive lady, and catch up to the wagon train on foot. It was estimated that there were times when Snodgrass covered half the distance from Ashcroft to Barkerville on foot.

# Gettin' Hitched

*Sometimes Frank and I had to improvise. This bride went to her Richfield wedding on horseback because the stagecoach couldn't go up the road. The groom had to walk.*

The secret of Snodgrass's success was not known: he was not handsome, he was of medium build, he had black beady eyes, and his nose deviated slightly to the left. Professor Huston said that for many years after, if you stopped at Clinton, 100 Mile House, or Deep Creek to get gas or whatever and if you mentioned the name Snodgrass, there was a hushed silence. If you looked closely at the young persons serving you, you would notice that they had beady black eyes and their nose deviated slightly to the left. So I went by the name Snodgrass. Three years later I changed my Barkerville persona and became Dr. Thomas Bell, the surgeon who was in charge of the Royal Cariboo Hospital in 1870—I was now both a real surgeon and an acting surgeon.

## Gettin' Hitched

One of Barkerville's attractive singers from the Theatre Royal was getting married and she wondered how she could be transported up to the courthouse at Richfield. I asked Frank about it and he said that he didn't go up that far with the stagecoach and that horses and wagons, or even buggies, were not allowed up the narrow road. I used to ride a saddle horse and drag a pack horse up there sometimes, so I told the young lady that anywhere I could go with a pack horse I would be glad to take her. We would make a comfortable throne for her on the top pack and she would ride up in style like a maharajah of India. The groom would have to walk.

They arranged for Joan Booth, marriage commissioner, to come from Quesnel, and the wedding party made its way up to the Richfield Courthouse on foot. The attractive bride rode side-saddle on old Barney; I led him on Chief. An officer from the Royal Engineers in dress uniform accompanied the bride, walking beside her and occasionally giving her a boost up when she started leaning too far to the port side.

The maid of honour was played by six-foot John Johnson in a white organdy gown, wig, and bouquet of wild flowers, riding on a little brown mule. As we were about to start off the procession, the little mule looked around and saw the goofy-looking creature on her back and promptly took off on a dead run and disappeared behind a freight shed. We finally got her back into the line and proceeded up the trail to Richfield. Everything went off according to schedule and it was a riotously funny affair.

## Skirt-Chasing, Barkerville Style

Hauling the gold shipment was a street performance, which the street actors tried to make a big thing of but which Frank and I thought was pretty phony. Once a week we would have to load the strongbox in the wagon at the stable office and haul it down the street to the Barnard Express office, all under armed escort with a bunch of street actors carrying phony old-time rifles gathered around us trying to look tough. None of the guns worked, and I think that none of those guys could hit a bull on the ass with a scoop shovel in any case.

For this occasion Ned Stout (Frank) had worked out a plan with the hookers, who stayed at the Nicol Hotel, and with Big Larry from the Sheepskin Claim, who also was one of the escorts for the gold. I was riding shotgun for Frank. When we got even with the Nicol Hotel, all these girlies came out on the balcony and put on a real siren's act, complete with striptease and cooing and oohing. Frank pulled the team over and handed his tie ropes to the closest pedestrian on the street. I threw down my gun and jumped off the wagon box, followed by Frank and Big Larry. We all made a run for the hotel door and up the stairs before the other guards knew what was going on. After they caught on, the other guys tried to follow us into the hotel and up the stairs, but we locked the door behind us. The crowd thought this was absolutely hilarious. Of the actors who took themselves overly seriously, some didn't catch on to what was happening until it was all over.

The co-ordinator of the street performers, which included us, was not too happy with this unrehearsed performance, but we didn't worry. Frank had a contract to supply and operate horse outfits, and I worked for him, not the co-ordinator. The Park Superintendent said that the only thing that was wrong with it was that he missed some of it.

After we put the wagon and the horses away, Frank and I retired to our private office at the stables and sat down for a drink of rum and a good laugh. We chuckled at intervals for the next week, thinking of those guys wondering what we were going to do next.

We usually managed to get a laugh somewhere during the day. On one occasion the CBC was making a movie in Barkerville and we became big-time movie stars. I had to take my saddle horse and pack horses through the creek several times so that they could pick up the sounds of my horses' shoes clattering on the rocks.

The whole business of street performing and movie making, and the people involved in it, was all a bit phony. In fact, everyone working in Barkerville, including ourselves, were phony. It was a different world in which we portrayed life as it was a hundred years ago. At the end of the summer season we were sorry to part. We had developed a real affection for the actors we worked with, though with some of them that was difficult. However, as I used to say to Frank, it was easier than working for a living.

The Barkerville actors took the gold shipment skit very seriously (top). Some hurdy-gurdy girls (like the ones on the right) helped Frank and I pull off the Nicol Street caper (bottom). The hookers on the balcony used their feminine wiles to lure us from the gold shipment, much to the actors' frustration.

Sometimes the rest of my family also played Barkerville characters. Here Judi Holley hams it up on the steps of the "Sporting House" (top).

Marissa and Brady haul water for Gramps— Frank Cushman—while he chops wood.

*While on the MacKenzie/Grease Trail, Toby Cave and I climbed to the Rainbow alpine. We are looking out over the Bella Coola Valley.*

## The Grease Trail

Another odyssey that I will mention only briefly is the trip Toby Cave and I took from Quesnel through the backcountry to Bella Coola on the Pacific Ocean during the summer of 1992. Toby was 71; I was 69. We followed the Grease Trail, which the Native people used to transport oolichan oil from the coast to the interior, where they traded it for elk and moose hides. It was on this trail, sometimes referred to as the MacKenzie Trail, that local Native people guided Alexander MacKenzie on his historic trip in 1793, the first trip by a white man across the North American continent. This trip was twelve years earlier than the much-publicized Lewis and Clark expedition on the U.S. side of the border.

We took our saddle horses and two pack horses and spent 30 days on the trail. Describing the whole trip would require another whole book. Anyone interested in the trip can see the photos we supplied for the pictorial at the Quesnel Tourist Info booth at LeBourdais Park at the entrance to the City of Quesnel.

We crossed and recrossed the Blackwater River, the Euchiniko and also the Upper Dean on our trek. We visited the Kluskus Village, Ulgatcho, and various Native camps along the way. We traversed the Rainbow Mountains, now encompassed in Tweedsmuir National Park; this included

*We started each day at 6 a.m. and spent the next 8 or 9 hours in the saddle (top). I'm standing in front of the Rainbow Mountains.*

*This is the Dean River canyon (bottom). The trail can be treacherous, but for the moderately experienced rider, this trip is without compare.*

*Toby leads the pack horse by Fish Lake. "I've been flying throughout this whole area for the better part of 30 years," Toby said of the trip. "But it's the first time I have ever seen the Rainbow Mountains from the ground. It's so different—so many colours. I guess that's why they call them the Rainbow Mountains."*

some of the wildest and untrammelled country in North America. Where we descended into Bella Coola Valley at Burnt Bridge Creek we dropped three thousand feet in four miles. After staying a day and two nights in Bella Coola to rest our horses and see the night life (it took half an hour) we climbed our horses back up "the precipice" out of the valley and followed our tracks back home.

We camped where there was good water and grass for the horses. On the way we met up with, and sometimes camped with, a group of British Army men. They were good fellows and traded us some of their army issue rations for some fresh Rainbow trout that we caught in the

*This is the Blackwater River at the Pan Meadow Crossing. The trail now bypasses the Kluskus village and joins with the original McKenzie/Grease trail at this point.*

Dean River. They nicknamed me Jacques Costeau, the great underwater adventurer, after I slipped—with all my gear—off an old slippery sloping footbridge into eight feet of water and took a little time to surface again. A six-foot tall Brigadier was half way into the water to rescue me when I surfaced, blowing and snorting and cursing beavers, environmentalists and anybody associated with them.

On our return, the Parks Board people subsidized us a little for reporting to them some bad spots within their park boundaries, and we appreciated it. The Forest Service also grubstaked us for our food that we ate on the trip along with some crushed oats for our horses. This was in return for supplying them with details of the current trail conditions and recommendations. We checked out various alternative routes for saddle horse use including crossing the Blackwater at Messue Crossing above the Upper Euchiniko Lake and following a trail above the Lakes and Blackwater River on the north side all the way down to what is now Ron Harrington's Ranch and guide headquarters.

This bypasses Kluskus Village completely and joins the main trail at Pan Meadows crossing. I don't know if that is what Kluskus chief Roger Jimmie wanted or not. I wonder if he knew himself. I asked him if he

*Toby and I turn back home, exploring alternate routes as we go. Here Toby crosses the Blackwater at the Messue Crossing, where the river breaks into three shallow channels.*

welcomed the traffic through Kluskus or not. He said he would rather not, so that's what we passed on to the Forest Service. I believe that he told them that he did not want white men travelling on any Indian trails. I notice that he and his band members felt quite free to use provincial highways on their way to town.

We arrived back at Norm Hjorth's place where we had left our pickup trucks and trailer. When we were breaking camp that morning it started to drizzle, the first rain we encountered during our 30 days on the trail. Among our recommendations to the Forest Service about the trail was that when crossing rivers you had to pay attention to weather and to how much rain was coming down, and how much snow was still on the higher mountains. These factors predicated how high the rivers would be at the crossings. There was plenty of swamp and muskeg to cross and areas of slippery bedrock, which wasn't too bad for hiking but could be deadly for shod horses. It was not a trail for novice riders with novice horses, but for anyone with a little bit of experience and a modicum of horse sense, it is a trail that is beyond compare. We enjoyed every minute of it.

## The Brahma Bull's Swan Dive

It was in May 1997, I think, that Bull-Riding Champion Darryl Mills from Fort St. John, and the Rodeo Club, held a bull-riding school in Quesnel. They needed a doctor in attendance for insurance purposes, so I volunteered. It was a good school, but a lot of the riders were pretty young, and some of them couldn't even ride a lively saddle horse, let alone a bucking, twisting Brahma. Anyway, there were a couple of severe injuries—a dislocated hip and a fractured femur—and I was glad I was there, if for no other reason than to save the injured riders from the overzealous treatment of the paramedics who were on the scene.

One young bull, a long-legged, big, black Brahma cross, evidently got tired of the scene. When he had bucked off his rider he loped over to the side of the arena and cleared the eight-foot fence like nothing at all, climbed up the embankment to the highway, and was last seen heading south. My daughter Mouse saw him just about at the Valhalla Motel.

At the two-hour noon break I jumped in my pickup and drove off to see if I could find where he went. Albert Gassoff had some cows at his place a half-mile south, but the bull had not showed up there. I turned off the highway and went down toward the Quesnel River on one of the old roads going that way. At the bottom of the hill I picked up his tracks and followed them upriver, past the stockcar raceway and heading up towards the Quesnel River Canyon. He looked to be moving right along. I did not have all day to spend, so I went back to the rodeo grounds and told the stock contractor where his bull was headed. The contractor and some friends apparently looked for the bull that evening, but lost his tracks. They did not seem too perturbed. The school wound up and everybody took off and nothing more was heard of the bull that played hooky until three or four weeks later.

Otto Siewert met up with him in the hayfield on his little homestead above the Quesnel River Canyon. I was not aware that Otto had such an aversion to bulls, but he was not comfortable with this uninvited guest and did not make him welcome. A couple of days later, Geoff Thomas told us that a schoolteacher had been hiking along the power line south of Otto's place and had the hell scared out of him by a big black bull. Some people at the bottom of Otto's trail, at the boat launch, said the teacher never stopped running all the way from the power line to the boat launch and that he was white as a ghost when he got there.

At that point I saddled a horse and rode up the power line on the east side of the lake, which is not far from our place, to see if I could pick up his tracks. It really wasn't a great concern of mine: it wasn't my bull. But I knew that my good friend Geoff had a herd of purebred Hereford

*Here are some real cowboys in action. These Chilcotin cowboys finally loaded this stubborn Brahma bull into the trailer after a successful escape.*

brood cows at his place not far off the power line, just three miles south, and the Burt boys had a bunch of Gelbeveh (exotic) cows at their place right on the power line. I was sure that they would not be happy for this big Brahma to be reorganizing their breeding program for them. I wanted to find out for them if he was heading their way.

The RCMP and Game Department boys told Otto to shoot the bull next time they met up, as it was illegal for him to be loose on the range. I had never hunted Brahma bulls before and it sounded like an interesting diversion. He was worth money to the stock contractor, though, so it would be better to catch him. I agreed to meet the cowboys at Murphy's Pub at 11 a.m., so I drove there with my truck and horse trailer with saddle horse inside.

At 1:30 p.m. (11 a.m. Chilcotin time) they showed up and I led them over to where I had last seen his tracks. I left for home, but they stayed and searched some more and finally caught up to him in the brush. They roped him, getting two ropes on him, and snubbed him up between two birch trees. They then got the four-wheel-drive truck and four-horse trailer backed in to where the bull was and started to load him. Otto Siewert, Albert Gassoff and two of his boys, and Eric Hyndman, who owned the truck and horse trailer, were there to help the two cowboys, along with four cow dogs. They had dragged him right up to the back of the trailer, but then the bull decided to take off. He broke one rope, knocked the tailgate wide open, knocked Albert Gassoff ass-over-teakettle, and took off north up the power line.

The two cowboys built new loops and took off after him. Their dogs were in hot pursuit, with one dog dragging from his tail and one hanging onto his nose. Even with the dogs slowing him down, the saddle horses couldn't catch him on the open power line. They followed him right to the drop-off, where he plunged full speed over the riverbank, all the way down to the river. He jumped in the Quesnel River below the canyon and swam across. They watched him climb out on the other side. The boys got their rig back out without wrecking it.

Next morning, armed with two new lariats, they drove around the north side of the river and went down at Bill Magnowski's place. They tracked the bull a short distance up the river, where they caught him in the thick brush and roped him again. I'll tell you, these guys were some kind of good cowboys, real Cariboo-Chilcotin cowboys. If you've ever tried to rope cows in the brush on rough ground you'll know what I'm talking about. It's one thing to do team roping in a nice smooth arena. I'm not even good at that. But to rope a 1,600- to 1,800-pound wild bull in the brush...that is something else again. I heard stories of some of these Chilcotin cowboys practising team roping on moose in earlier days. This would be on a par.

Anyhow, they snubbed this Brahma bull up to a couple of trees, then got a skidder to brush out a road down to where the bull was. After getting him safely into the trailer and tied down, they pulled the trailer back up the hill with the skidder. When they got back up to the farmyard they hooked Eric's truck back on, jumped their saddle horse in the trailer's back compartment, threw their four dogs into the pickup, thanked everyone for helping, and headed down the road. I don't think there are many cowboys like those boys anywhere in existence.

## Riding with a Cowboy Surgeon

One nice summer day a young lady and I went for a horseback ride up on the mountain above our place on the east side of Dragon Lake. The occasion was her twentieth birthday and the anniversary of the surgical procedure we had performed on her when she was two hours old and weighed about four pounds. Today she was a pleasant, attractive girl with a normal appearance, as well as being a good rider. I remembered that morning twenty years earlier quite well, but I don't think she did.

I got called to the delivery room in maternity that morning where one of the guys, Dr. Bill McIntyre, I believe, had just delivered a baby. It was obvious the baby had serious problems. I had never seen anything like this, not even at the Children's Hospital in Montreal. But I had heard of it, so I knew what it was. And more important, I had recently read a paper in the *Annals of Surgery* outlining a new and successful technique of looking after these babies.

The baby had a condition called Gastroschisis, which described in ordinary English means that a segment of the abdominal wall did not develop in utero, so that there was nothing to hold the innards inside. This baby was born sort of inside-out. In earlier days, attempts to surgically correct the problem by stretching the skin and sewing it over the protruding viscera (innards) had been unsuccessful because they placed the abdominal contents under too much pressure. The viscera would not tolerate this, and all the babies died.

But two surgeons in Philadelphia got a different idea. They placed a silastic (stretchy) chimney over the protruding stomach, bowel, etc., and stitched the edge of the chimney to the edge of the defect in the abdominal wall with a watertight running stitch. After this was stitched into place they flushed off the previously exposed innards with sterile saline and twisted the top of the bag closed, tying it with a rubber band. The baby's management included giving the top of the bag a couple of twists every day or so as the contents would tolerate the pressure. In a few days the abdominal contents would be all inside and it only required a few stitches to close the remaining defect. These surgeons reported good results and their little patients survived.

So we got the infant to the operating room, Dr. Bill got a minute anaesthetic tube in place, and we carried out the procedure described by the Philadelphians. We did not have a silastic tube available, which would have been more durable, so we improvised with a sterilized polyethylene colostomy bag and cut and tailored it to size and shape. We kept the baby in an incubator in the nursery for a few days, then flew her down to the Vancouver Children's Hospital under care of pediatric surgeon Dr. Phil Ashmore. They had more appropriate-sized equipment as well as expertise in this kind of project. Dr. Ashmore gave her good care and it was not too long before the baby was back in Quesnel, home with her very capable mother. I found out that there were a total of nineteen cases of gastroschisis at the Vancouver Children's Hospital since it opened, and this was the first one that had been successfully diagnosed and operated on outside of greater Vancouver.

Now we were having a pleasant ride on the mountain, discussing her future, her upcoming wedding, and plans for a family. This was one of the occasions when the many years of training seemed to be completely worthwhile. And I was grateful for the help and expertise of the nursing staff and my medical associates. These fancy jobs don't go so well unless there are good people working together.

*Being able to go horseback riding with former patients makes everything I've done worthwhile.*

# Epilogue

I will append to this account a few vignettes of people and places that may not have received their due in the main account.

My father also had a quiet, but sometimes earthy sense of humour. In describing one of our neighbour's culinary delights, he said that one day he gave some of it to the dog and the dog turned around and licked his butt to take the dirty taste out of his mouth.

My Irish mother had a store of good, practical Irish sayings such as, "If you can't say something good about somebody, don't say anything at all." She kept our family together as long as she lived. After she died we tended to drift apart. After a mother of a large family dies, the survivors should nominate one of their number whose job it will be to keep them all in touch with each other—or perhaps they should take turns.

C.D. Hoy, founder of C.D. Hoy and Co. General Store in Quesnel and a Cariboo photographer in the 1910s, had a good sense of humour. Someone was talking to C.D. about another Chinese man, Bill Hong, from Wells. Bill was a merchant and businessman who was a good guy, but he had the damndest way of talking and was very difficult to understand. This was mentioned in the discussion.

C.D. said, "You think he hard to understand in English, you should try him in Chinese."

Bill Hong in Wells, like C.D. Hoy and John A. Fraser in Quesnel, grubstaked a lot of men who were down on their luck, with very little said or known about it, but I think they did not lose out too often in the long run. Henry Rippen, an old-timer in Quesnel, now dead, told of how he arrived in Prince George on the Grand Trunk Railway, en route to Quesnel. The railway did not join Prince George and Quesnel yet, nor was there a road. Henry made a raft and loaded all his belongings on it. He would raft to Quesnel. No one told him of the rough Cottonwood Canyon, and when unsuspecting Henry hit this stretch of water, his raft upset and he lost all of his belongings—bedroll, rifle, campstove, everything—in the river, but managed to get ashore himself.

He followed the riverbank to Quesnel, and when he got there he was destitute. Even his immigration papers were gone. He walked down Front Street to Fraser's Store, where he met John A. Fraser, the owner, and told him his story. John A. told him to pick up what he needed: clothes, blankets, tools, a shovel, and a grubstake. Then he told him to hike back up the river to Cottonwood Canyon, about 25 miles, and there he should find a man working a claim on the river. He further told him that the claim just above this was open and to tell the man to show him where this claim was. He said to stake it and get to work on it. He could come back and pay John A. whenever he had made some money. And he did. I operated on Henry for gallstones in Quesnel when he was in his 80s, and he lived several years after that, still grateful to John A. Fraser.

That is the way the merchants and other businesspeople in this frontier country operated in those early days. If they had clothing and food in their store they wouldn't let a man freeze or starve to death. They couldn't make any money dealing with a frozen corpse, so why not give the man a chance? I think some of us who grew up in the Cariboo inherited that philosophy. I had absolutely no time for some of our hired doctors in later years who refused to treat a patient because he had no money. If the doctor didn't make enough treating his paying patients to be able to treat a few indigent patients free, he must not have been working hard enough. I did it. I didn't get rich, but I survived. I was broke when I came into this country and I will be broke when I go out. But I have enjoyed many good times and have had many good friends, and those are things no amount of money can buy.

# Dr. Donald Alexander Holley

## 1924–2000

## In Memoriam

*Dr. Holley passed away on October 5, 2000, at the age of 76. What follows is the eulogy by Dr. Geoff Thomas given at his funeral. With warm humour reminiscient of Al's, Dr. Thomas tells us how Dr. Holley was a storyteller who became "larger than life."*

I had the honour and privilege to be a friend of Al Holley. I can see from all the people here that it was an honour and privilege shared by many. Your presence here indicates the high esteem in which he was held.

Al was born in Saskatoon, Saskatchewan in 1924 and at the age of thirteen was on a train to B.C. After initially settling in the North Thompson country, he arrived with his family in Quesnel in 1939. School in Quesnel was followed by Grade 13 in Trail. He obtained a Masters of Science at the U of A. In 1951 he graduated from medical school in Edmonton, then he interned in Victoria at the Royal Jubilee Hospital. In 1952 Al arrived in the Northwest Territories for a year at Fort Rae. There he provided medical care for all and sundry and was responsible for a significant decrease in the Native death rate. Residencies in General Surgery followed in Montreal, New York City, the Cleveland Clinic, and Calgary. In addition to his surgical fellowship in the Royal College in Canada, he was a Fellow of the American College of Surgeons.

When Al arrived in Quesnel in 1957, he soon started the Holley Clinic where he practised general surgery until his retirement in 1984. Al's retirement simply shifted his attention from medicine to his first love—horses. Along with his good friend Frank Cushman, he ran the stagecoach and delivery wagons in Barkerville under his alias Snodgrass.

But medicine pulled him back, and in the nineties Al returned to G.R. Baker to act as a surgical assistant. He continued this until his stroke in 1997. In spite of this debilitating illness he was able to spend the next two years writing his autobiography Don't Shoot From The Saddle: Chronicles of a Frontier Surgeon. He finished the final edit just prior to his last hospitalization.

I first met Al in 1975 when I came to Quesnel to do a clinical clerkship. His ability to make a complicated procedure or case look routine and his natural teaching ability were instrumental in directing my professional life.

Al was proof that you didn't have to be in an ivory tower in order to practice outstanding and frontline medicine. Early on he established an ICU in Quesnel, one of B.C.'s first. As a general surgeon he was able to do just about anything as many of you can probably attest.

One of Al's strongest professional habits was his constant quest for knowledge. He annually was off to spend a week here or there, often at the Cleveland Clinic, to update or learn a new skill—all for the betterment of his patients and this community. Al understood the need for CME long before most of us knew what it was.

But as I said earlier, medicine was only one part of Al's life. Among other things, he was a Justice of the Peace in the Northwest Territories, a cowboy, an author, a stagecoach driver and actor in Barkerville, a historian, an artist, a hunter, an explorer, a rodeo doctor, a dogmusher, a train robber, a lieutenant in the RCA Medical Corp, a husband, a father, and a grandfather.

Al had a storyteller's ability to captivate an audience. First the clearing of his throat, then, with eyes twinkling, he would give a history of everyone he was about to talk about. His stories were often a reflection of Al himself and generally went to the very essence of people. He had the unique ability to laugh, not only at what life tossed up but also at himself. In spite of hearing the same story a hundred times, I kick myself for not recording them—all were unique in their own way.

A lot about Al was larger than life:

his size 13 custom-made riding boots;

his lifelong love affair with his Indian sweater and toque;

his bearclaw slippers;

his enjoyment of a cheery little fire;

his comfortable ranch home on Dragon Lake welcoming any and everybody;

McGregor, his talking bear;

his ability to break bones at a rate exceeded only by the Mafia;

his surgical ability extended to animals as well as people in his early years;

hot rums no matter the outside temperature;

his love of riding a good horse on a bright fall day;

the scientist in him often coming out while mixing drinks like rum and tang—a favourite

his harmonica playing with endless renditions of *You are My Sunshine*—the only song he was able to play, but he loved music, especially live performances and he was involved early on with Music in the Park;

his own time-clock—Al was never in a hurry;

his love of rodeo—he was a member of the Quesnel Rodeo Club, and as the rodeo doctor he reserved specific treatment for rodeo cowboys, usually in a 26-ounce dosage;

his love of reading—anything from poetry to the latest medical journal, even after his stroke;

an immense appetite—even when he was ill he was always worried about his next meal;

his love of pie, especially banana cream, but he had a dislike, or so he claimed, of cake;

dogsledding around Dragon Lake;

the overproof classic—the race between the Holleys and the Moffats that pitted Al and his dogs against Tom's horse and cutter—this event was curtailed when Al forgot that his dogsled was tied to the back of his truck, drove into town, and then spent the next several weeks collecting dog harnesses off of Front street; and

his love of a good joke—whether he was telling one, playing one, or was the recipient of a practical joke.

Al was the original recycler: he never met a nail or fencing staple that he couldn't straighten out and use again.

Al was not a man who minced his words. What he said was what he thought, no more no less; even if at times he had to extract a foot out of his mouth at a later date. One of his last written requests was that there be no wake, "I would not like any wake at least not at my house, I don't want to supply any booze unless I am going to be at the party to help drink it."

We all have lost an important part of our lives. Al meant different things to so many people. A man of contradictions: equally at ease in the OR at the Cleveland Clinic or rounding up horses out at Chezacut; a man who could do the most exacting technically demanding surgery but was no Mr Fix-it at home; a man who dedicated his life to improving the health and quality of life for others, himself suffering a debilitating stroke. No man so vital, so active, so strong should suffer, so it was a blessing in his passing.

But what a man, so self-effacing, so caring, and what a great set of memories he left us. He lent a great blessing and fullness to our lives. Al, you were many things in your life but most of all you were a friend. We'll miss you.

I finally get my chance to drive the herd into town (top).

My daughter Marissa ("Mouse") shows off our catch while on a family fishing trip on the way to River City. We caught fourteen trout by casting from the shore (right).

Outdoor living has its advantages (left). On a trip by Riske Creek we found a soda-water spring. It went great with scotch.

*Judi and I were married in 1979 and enjoyed rides together until I became disabled.*

# Index

185

Prince George  19, 44, 121, 122, 124, 128, 133, 177
Prince Rupert  19
Prophet River  146
Public Health  142
Purden Lake  44
Putnam, Bob  50
Putnam, Jean  50, 51
Putnam, Mrs.  46

Quebec  86
Queen Mary Veterans Hospital  107, 108
Quesnel  26, 27, 29-31, 34, 36, 38, 39, 42, 45, 111-117, 121-125, 128, 132, 134-137, 139, 140, 142, 145, 152, 155-158, 163, 172-175, 177, 178, 180
Quesnel airport  42
*Quesnel Observer*  142
Quesnel River  27, 30, 31, 36, 38, 132, 172, 174
Quesnel River Canyon  31, 172
Quesnel Rodeo Club  172, 181

Rabbit Hill Presbyterian Church  46
Railway bulls  18
Rainbow Mountains  135, 167
Rancherie Reserve 31, 32
Rankine, Dr. Jim  112
RCAF  82, 122, 181
RCAMC  108
RCMP  50, 66, 82, 86-89, 91, 93-95, 99, 101, 102, 106, 115, 124, 125, 133, 136, 139, 158, 173
Red Bluff Hill  27
Red Pass Junction  19
Richfield  163
Rippen, Henry  177
Riske Creek  183
Riviere des Roches  67
Rock Creek  51
Rocky Mountain House  61, 62
Rocky Mountains  19, 20
Roman Catholic nuns  86
Ron Wiwchar  149
Ross River  77, 79, 80
Royal Alexandria Hospital  69
Royal Cariboo Hospital  163
Royal Jubilee Hospital  85, 180
Roylance, Ron  51, 52, 53

Russell, Gordon  58
Russell Lake  96, 97, 101

Salmo  59
Sanschagrin, Maurice and Marie  89
Sargent, R.  85
Saskatchewan  9, 15, 26, 41, 46, 48, 55, 63, 68, 126, 137
Saskatoon  9, 15, 16, 17, 18, 180
Schottische  69
Scotland  117, 131
Scotty Creek  76, 77
Screaming Six  53
Sherbinnin, John  54
Sherbinnin, Tanya  54
Sheridan Lake  26
Shot-on-both-Sides, Chief Charlie  61
Siewert, Otto  172, 173
Sikanni Chief  73
Skip, Lee  125, 126
Sladen, Joe  121
Slave River  67
Slavey  87
Slemon Lake  97, 101
Slim Creek  44
Smith, Batnunni  158
Smith, Larry  151
Smith, Snuffy  53
Smoke Valley  154
Smoky Gray  106
Snag  75
Snare River  96, 97, 99, 100
Snodgrass  160, 161, 163, 180
Snowshoe  44
Soda Creek  26
Spencer, Alf  127
Spencer-Dickie Drugs  127, 139
Spences Bridge  47
Sporting House  166
Squeaky  102-105
Squinas Meadows  135
St. Stephen's College  56
Standbridge, Bruce  38
Stewart  59, 82
Stinson, Sergeant  158
Stojan, R.  85
Stony Rapids  67
Stout, Ned  160, 164
Strawberry, Jim  65
streptomycin  87, 88, 90, 91
stump ranch  26, 27, 32, 41, 137

# The Author

Dr. Donald Alexander Holley travelled by horse, train, plane, and dogsled through the Arctic, the Cariboo, the prairies, New York City and Montreal as he trained to become a surgeon. He served his home community of Quesnel as a surgeon since 1957—that is, whenever he wasn't hunting, fishing or riding the range.

Dr. Holley created B.C.'s first Intensive Care Unit at the G. R. Baker Memorial Hospital. In 1981, Al "Doc" Holley became the president of the B.C. Surgical Society. He retired in the late 80s. Al Holley then started a new career as an actor in Barkerville, playing a teamster, "Snodgrass," and the town doctor, "Dr. Bell." Dr. Holley passed away on October 5, 2000. He was on his horse as long as he was able.